For Fred
Good eating

Best wishes,
Jim Thomson

Tough Guys Don't Dice

Tough Guys Don't Dice

A Cookbook for Men Who Can't Cook

James A. Thorson

William Morrow and Company, Inc.
New York

Endpaper photographs of the author by James R. Belt

Library of Congress Cataloging-in-Publication Data
Thorson, James A., 1946–
Tough guys don't dice / by James A. Thorson.
p. cm.
Includes index.
ISBN 0-688-08220-3
1. Cookery, beginners I. Title.
TX652.T463 1989
641.5'61—dc19 88-37592
CIP

Printed in the United States of America

First Edition

1 2 3 4 5 6 7 8 9 10

BOOK DESIGN BY JAYE ZIMET

FOR JUDY, WHO KEEPS ME COOKING

Contents

Introduction

If you're like me, the movie *Mr. Mom* sent you straight up the wall. Gone are the days when Daddy in the kitchen evokes a cutsie image of the inept American male fumbling through the kitchen, making a royal mess as he tries to boil water without setting the house on fire. TV commercials are even worse. Men, we don't have to put up with this horseshit. There's no reason why a man of average intelligence should have to be ashamed of his ability to cook. We're socialized to take mastery on the football field, in the office, and on the highway.

Our sisters have been bitching and moaning for years that they were taught how to bake apple pies while we were out building character and important business networks for the future while playing cowboys and Indians. I'm not sure I swallow that; I went back to my hometown not too long ago and downed a few beers with the guys I used to run around with, and it turned out to be a pretty sorry network. Two were unemployed, one had an assembly-line job, and the one who looked like he was going on to great things worked nights keeping track of the pressure gauges on a boiler. The most successful one of the lot had taken over his father's landscaping business and spends his time supervising a crew of liberal-arts graduate students who mow lawns for him. None seemed to be in a position to hire me as a consultant or to come up with a reasonable speaker's fee, so it looks like my important contacts from the playing fields of my youth aren't going to produce, unless I want to cut grass for a living.

The point is, *we* were the ones who got the short end of the stick. Being able to bake an apple pie can, in fact, be useful. I've yet to find a use for skill at cowboys and Indians. While we were being socialized into taking on manly tasks, our sisters were learning important survival skills. Maybe they regret it now, but at least they learned how to do a few things right.

I remember when O'Reilly, my high school biology lab partner, showed me how he cooked his lunch. He'd take a can of ravioli and put it, unopened, into a 400-degree oven for twenty minutes. Exercising reasonable caution while opening the hot can, he got away with it the first few times. Then there was the time he got a phone call and left the can in the oven for forty minutes. Don't try this at home. The first puncture the can opener made allowed a jet of steam and boiling ravioli to hit the ceiling of his mother's kitchen with truly astonishing velocity. His mother was . . . *distressed* when she came home and found the mess, but she never took O'Reilly by the hand to teach him a few simple things to do in the kitchen. You didn't teach boys such things; boys were supposed to be interested in baseball and science projects. Actually O'Reilly was interested in beer and pussy. He's a stockbroker in Dallas now, and, the last time I saw him, he was still interested in beer and pussy. He still can't cook.

The week before I took off for college, my mother showed me how to iron a shirt. God bless the woman. After about twenty minutes, I realized that there's no mystery to ironing a shirt, any idiot can do it. Why such a simple manual skill had not been a part of my liberal education until then escapes me. Permanent-press shirts are great, but I still know which end of an iron goes first, and it's something that has come in handy over the years.

I got over thinking about domestic chores as sissy stuff that's just for girls early on when I took a part-time job in a bakery. The professional bakers, most of whom seemed to be former German war prisoners, were big, tough guys. What amazed me is how fast these guys moved; there was no farting around in that bakery. They had skill at their business, they were sure of their moves, and they had pride in their work. Toting 100-pound flour sacks up a flight of stairs, or getting on the other side of a 300-pound tub of bread dough and swinging it with your partner up onto a wooden table were not jobs for sissies. Those guys gave me a respect for hard work well done that I've carried with me all my life. And I've never been afraid of baking stuff since that experience.

My wife and I split up the work around the house some years back. I'm a pretty good cook, so I do most of the kitchen stuff. Judy takes care of the laundry. Neither of us cleans the house. It's a fair deal: She brings home a good paycheck, and she works harder on her job than I do on mine. Why should I expect her to do all the work at home?

My next-door neighbor, Richard, was a lazy asshole who would spend his entire weekend curled up on the sofa under a comforter while his wife, who was a jewel, ran herself ragged. Richard was maybe a special case: He couldn't even motivate himself to go look at houses with her, or to take care of the kids while *she* was out looking for one. She'd have to pack up the kids in the VW and go off while he was watching Daffy Duck on Saturday mornings. God forbid that he should go to the store to buy his own beer. She came home one day and told him she'd bought a house, and he said, "Okay. How about bringing me a can of beer?" Now, the hell of it is, Richard thought of himself as a sportsman, and if you were to ask him what activities he enjoyed, he'd have said boating and fishing (he kept an old canoe upside down in the backyard). His hobby really was sitting on his ass. Lucy never put her foot down, but I think he should have motivated himself a little better. You don't want to lose a good woman like that.

Now, this book is not intended to be a manifesto for the androgynous male, and I don't have a subscription to *Ms.* You make your own deal with your wife. Maybe you don't want to take over all the cooking. Perhaps you keep her happy in other ways. It could be that you just don't want to feel so lost and alone the week she goes to stay with Mother. Or maybe she kicked you out years ago and you're tired of TV dinners and Big Macs.

We're going on the assumption that your mother didn't teach you any more about cooking than mine did. I had to learn by doing. And I was surprised how easy it is to look good and eat well without working very hard. Just don't be intimidated. Cooking most things takes less skill than tuning my old Chevy. I'm going to throw in a lot of my own recipes that I've developed over the years, but this isn't your regular cookbook, where they assume you know how to separate egg yolks from the whites. We'll focus on *how* to cook, and I'll throw in some tricks I've picked up over the years. Finally, we're not going to try anything too fancy. My eyes start to glaze over at the point where Julia Child sticks the knife up the fish's ass and starts to rip away while her Kapernsauce is simmering on the back burner. None of that. We'll take maximum advantage of the stuff on the shelf that's been designed to take the work *out* of cooking. Instead of exotic stuff, we'll look at how to prepare good, solid food and plenty of it. Even a Thanksgiving turkey dinner is a no-sweat proposition if you go at it the right way.

CHAPTER 1

Breakfast

▸ STARTING WITH BASICS: THE EGG

I think eggs are wonderful. Judy says eggs are icky. Whatever turns you on. She'll eat an occasional egg when it comes as part of a salad, but she has sort of a hopeless look on her face when I serve them for breakfast. In most cases, I let Judy, Bob, and Pete forage for themselves at breakfast time, and our household goes through truckloads of cornflakes and Cheerios each year. But when I'm cooking for myself or for me and the boys, eggs are on the breakfast menu.

The egg is a dandy source of protein; it's compact, easy to store, and lasts for weeks when properly stored (don't keep them in the egg thing in the refrigerator door, by the way, that shakes them up and leaves them warmer than they should be; keep them in the carton on the bottom shelf). Dollar for dollar, eggs are the cheapest source of protein you can buy. Lay off of them if you must hold your cholesterol down; but an egg now and again isn't going to harm most people.

▸ BOILING THE EGG

Perhaps this sounds pretty basic to you, and if you cook much at all yourself, you may want to flip ahead. However, it's amazing to me that there are so many people who don't know how to boil an egg.

The quickest way to crack an egg is to dump a cold egg into a pot of boiling water. The insides start to seep out of the crack and make your water all cruddy and your egg look like a mutant. If you want a boiled egg to come out whole, gently place the eggs you're going to cook in the bottom of the pot and fill it with hot water from the tap so that there's enough to cover them. (Contrary to the fervent belief of my old friend Huff, hot water will boil more quickly than cold water. Conversely, cold water will freeze more quickly than hot water. Learn these principles.) Heat the pot of eggs and water until the water boils, cover the pot, and turn off the heat (or turn it to low if you want hard-boiled eggs). Now the period of waiting begins.

If you like your yolks still runny, take the eggs out of the hot water after about four minutes. Semisoft but still sticky, about six or seven minutes. Hard like an Easter egg? Ten minutes at least.

Jonathan Swift once satirized warring political groups as big-endians, those who like to crack their egg on the big end, and small-endians (he got into hot water himself for being a smartass). I have to side with the small-endians. They seem to peel better that way. Now, here's a good trick: Don't toss the hot water out. Instead, fish the eggs out with a pair of tongs and run cold water over them. This will shrink the cooked egg inside the shell. Then, immediately before peeling, briefly dip the egg back into the hot water; this will expand the shell away from the cooked egg and make peeling simple. Try it. It works.

15•BREAKFAST

▸ THE SCRAMBLED EGG

Scrambling an egg is about the easiest thing you can do in the kitchen, and if you screw up on this, perhaps there really is little hope.

My friend Chuck used to help out at our church breakfasts. He'd bring his own eggbeater from home and, after he'd cracked a couple dozen eggs into a big bowl, he'd sit there and crank the damn thing until his wrist was sore. We'd be done with the bacon and the sausage and yell over to him, "Chuck, we're ready to cook the eggs, bring them over already!" But he'd just keep cranking, and he wouldn't turn his egg-and-milk blend loose until the whole thing was perfectly mixed, about the consistency of 40-weight motor oil. Chuck died of a heart attack last year at the age of forty-seven, so you can see what happens to fussbudgets.

It happens that there's no reason at all to whip your eggs in a bowl; they're going to get scrambled around in the frying pan anyway, so why go to the extra work? Put a little oil or bacon grease (about a teaspoonful) in the frying pan. I like the kind of pan that has a no-stick surface, and the Silverstone ones seem to be an improvement over the earlier kinds of Teflon. If you're using a pan with a no-stick surface, you'll find it much easier to clean afterward, but be careful to use a rubber spatula to stir the eggs with so you don't chip the surface of the pan. Do your scrambled eggs over medium heat. Crack the eggs into the oiled pan and add a couple ounces of milk. I ran out of milk one time and tried adding water, and I think I'd have been better off adding nothing at all. Stir up the eggs and milk with your spatula so that the yolks break, and then keep stirring, going around the edges particularly well. The trick to a good scrambled egg is to not overcook and dry it out. Take the eggs out while they're still a little moist. If you really want to put on the dog, add some small cubes of Velveeta about a minute before the eggs are done, being careful to stir it in well. Don't add the Velveeta too early, or it will separate into its component parts rather than just melt, and you'll find yourself with well-cooked eggs that have water seeping out of them.

▸ THE FRIED EGG

Frying a good egg is a little trickier than boiling or scrambling, but I've got a surefire method for coming up with good-looking fried eggs with no trouble at all. I prefer to use the same frying pan that I've cooked my bacon in, so there's only one pan to wash. Pour out all of the bacon grease; the thin film that remains will be enough to fry your eggs in. Break the eggs gently into the hot pan, then pour in about a tablespoon of water. Cover immediately and turn off the heat if you're using an electric stove (there's enough heat left in the element to fry the eggs) or put it on very low heat if you're using a gas stove. The steam from the water boiling in the hot frying pan will cook the top of the eggs, so you never have to flip them over and get the tops all funny-looking or break the yolks. Depending on how hot your pan was (don't use one that's too hot, or you'll have brown crust on the bottoms of your fried eggs), the eggs will cook in the time it takes you to butter your toast. You'll have to experiment a little with this to get it just to your taste. I like my yolks runny so I can swap the toast around in them, which really grosses Judy out. If you like firm yolks, just let them sit on the heat a little longer under the cover. Either way, you don't have to flip them, and the tops come out all pretty and white.

▸ THE MICROWAVED EGG

There are any number of busybodies who will tell you that they can make wonderful eggs in the microwave. They're full of shit.

▸ THE POACHED EGG

Poaching an egg the right way goes beyond the scope of this book. After all, we're trying to make cooking easy, not hard. There is a way to cheat on poached eggs, however, and that's by cooking them the same way I've described frying eggs, only breaking them into those little tin rings that you can put on the surface of the frying pan. I'm not sure why anyone would want to do this, because cleaning the rings can be a pain in the ass. The only reason to poach an egg is so that you can put it on top of corned beef hash, and you can do the same thing with a fried egg, so what the hell. Which brings us to:

▸ CORNED BEEF HASH

No one in his right mind would buy a corned beef brisket, bake it, and then shred it up just for hash. The canned corned beef hash you can buy in the store is just as good as the stuff you could make yourself anyway, and a sight less trouble. There is a trick, however, to using this stuff the right way, because it's crumbly at room temperature and a mess to work with. I like my hash in little hills with the top squished down to make space for an egg. Getting it to stay up in little hills is more sculpting than I have time for, so I do this: Keep the canned hash in the refrigerator; this will keep it nice and firm. When you open the can, take off both the top and the bottom, so that you can shove the whole congealed can of hash out one end of the can as a solid mass. Then cut the cylinder of hash into thirds or quarters, place each piece on a cookie sheet, and mush down the middles with a tablespoon. Bake in a 350-degree oven for about ten minutes, finishing off with the oven on broil for the last two minutes. Do your eggs in the meantime, slip them into the little volcanoes, and you've got a fancy breakfast.

▸ TOAST

You already know how to make toast.

▸ FRENCH TOAST

French toast is easier than pancakes and tastes better. Just whip up a couple of eggs in a bowl along with a couple ounces of milk; I whip the eggs with a fork, using a lateral wrist action. It's a lot easier to clean a fork than an eggbeater. I add a touch of cinnamon, maybe a quarter teaspoon, to give it some zip. Some people add a quarter teaspoon of salt, but I can't taste any difference. If you want to get fancy, you can put all this stuff in a blender and get it nice and frothy, but that's not necessary. Dip your bread into the egg mixture and fry on a lightly greased griddle at medium-high heat. For a different taste, try whole wheat bread instead of white. Save a step and grease the griddle with margarine and you won't have to butter your French toast; just be careful not to get it too hot, because margarine turns brown and tastes funny if it burns.

▸ PANCAKES

Pancakes are what you cook when you want French toast but are out of bread. I wouldn't bother buying one of the pancake mixes in the store; Bisquick is pretty much the same stuff and is handy for other things as well. I follow the recipe on the box, but I add extra milk because I like thin pancakes. Another tip: I use a square griddle that's pretty much like a flat frying pan with a Silverstone surface. They're pretty cheap and warp after a while, so about every two years I throw the old one out and get a new one. After you spoon the batter onto the hot griddle—about two or three tablespoons per pancake—lift up the griddle and swirl it around horizontally to spread the mixture out evenly and get thin pancakes. (If you like your pancakes like pillows, don't do this.) Have the oven hot, about 350 degrees, with a cookie sheet in it, so you'll have a place to keep the early pancakes warm while you're cooking the others. Nothing is so flat as a cold pancake. This is a good thing to remember when you're cooking French toast, too.

▸ HASH BROWNS

Hash browns are more trouble than they're worth.

SOME FURTHER THOUGHTS ON ▸ BREAKFAST

Breakfast is a nice thing to have late at night as well as at the usual time, but it's especially nice on a weekend morning to bring it in and lay around in bed with your wife and fiddle with each other. If you're going to all the trouble to serve your wife breakfast in bed, go the extra mile and shave and brush your teeth. It's these little extra touches that mean so much. Actually you don't have to *cook* breakfast. A toasted English muffin, juice, and coffee is plenty good enough. Sausages or bacon add a nice touch, as does a grapefruit half. I've gotten into the habit of having orange juice when I eat bacon or sausage; a nutrition professor told me once that the citrus counteracts the nitrites in the smoked meat. I wouldn't swear to it, but he usually knew what he was talking about.

A nice breakfast is one of those big caramel-nut rolls split in half; put a pat of butter on each half and stick it in the microwave (or the broiler of your oven) for half a minute. Then sprinkle a little cinnamon sugar over the melted butter. First-rate. Another good alternative to the usual is to half-toast your split English muffin, then put a thin slice of cheese on each half and broil it until the cheese melts a little.

Judy, who finds eggs to be icky, and who wouldn't get

within ten feet of a glob of corned beef hash, actually *likes* grapefruit. This is nothing against her character; she's a fine person, really. A lusty wench as well. Liking grapefruit is, to me, inexplicable. Its sole virtue, as far as I can see, is that it's about the same size as a sixteen-inch softball. Sixteen-inch softball is popular in my native city, Chicago. I've not seen it played elsewhere. Apropos of this, early on in our marriage, I pelted Judy with several grapefruits (she can't catch worth a damn). She's *still* pissed about this. One of the reasons that we've been married for over twenty years is that I've refrained from further grapefruit pelting. Got it out of my system, so to speak. At any rate, I admire agronomists who have been able to make a grapefruit pink. Now, if they could only develop one that tastes like something other than a grapefruit.

I'm firmly against toaster waffles as a matter of policy. They just don't taste like waffles. My friend Joe the Bookie, who lives alone, keeps his betting slips in the waffle box in the freezer. The cops know he's booking bets, but they can never find his records. Joe's got the right idea for the proper use for a box of frozen waffles.

Making breakfast is so easy that it really isn't cooking per se, but it's something that's good to get you started and familiar with the kitchen. Practice up and try different things; get creative. Once you feel comfortable with whipping up a little breakfast, you'll be getting your moves down and you'll notice that you start to get efficient. Now, on to bigger things.

CHAPTER 2

Lunch

▸ EXCELLING WITH LUNCH

Dependency is a drag, for either sex. The purpose of lunch is to give even the most dependent of do-nothing husbands a chance to fend off starvation. Anybody can make lunch.

Which brings up a point that I might as well pause and expand upon (I do stray from the point now and then, as my students are wont to remind me): Being helpless is unattractive.

Florence King wrote a dandy book a few years back about the helpless Southern-belle type who would invariably get a man to "do" for her. This is, of course, the flip side of the man who can do nothing for himself. Neither is an estimable sight.

My sister's friend Kathy got married right out of high school; this would have been in, say, about 1952. Kathy never, to the best of my knowledge, has given a thought to either work or higher education. She married a guy who went on to med school and then became a small-town physician. Being a doctor's wife in a small town was a good job. I remember a woman in Asheville, North Carolina, who won a seat on the city council with that sole qualification. Well, Kathy was able to lord it over the other women and generally be a big frog in a small pond. When the host dies, however, it's bad for the parasite, and the doctor kicked off several years back. Over thirty years of a dependent relationship have made Kathy into a cripple, and she's not been able to do anything since but spend up the life insurance. She's stuck.

Women in the current generation are playing by a new set of rules, thank God. A Nebraska farmer who was ahead of his time was quoted in our local paper, responding to why he had spent the money to send his seven daughters to college back in Depression days: "So they wouldn't become slaves to the sons of my neighbors."

Well, dependency is a mantle I'm glad to see people throw off. One ought to know how to make one's way in the world. This goes for men as well as women. Men ought to help out, for sure. But they ought to be able to feed themselves if they're alone, as well. That's why God created lunch.

Most men are really good at lunch and probably have been experimenting with sandwiches for years. Even the most inept can slap a few pieces of bologna between two slices of bread, maybe with a little mustard or some mayonnaise, and *voilà,* there's lunch. If you've progressed to toasting the bread and adding lettuce on your own, then take pride, my man. You have natural skills that should be cultivated, and you're already operating at a higher level than 80 percent of the cafeteria workers in the nation.

If you've had any success at all at making yourself a snack, most likely it's been something that might be included in a lunch, so you're on home ground here. Since we've got something to work with, I won't get too hung up on basics—just throwing in a few tips to make things easier—before moving on to more complex things.

Trivial Pursuit question: What kind of sandwich was it that the fourth earl of Sandwich had during his card game? Answer: roast beef. Thus, one of the neatest and handiest blessings to come to mankind was developed: two pieces of bread with stuff in between.

What you put between the two slices of bread is up to you, and an astonishing variety of different things have gone into sandwiches during the years. Peanut butter and jelly has provided strength to a nation for generations. Salami on rye. Ham and cheese. The hot dog. These are things that have made our democracy great. When we think of lunch, we think of the great American sandwich.

When I got to Hong Kong after three weeks in the People's Republic of China, the first thing I got was a cheeseburger. Neither bread nor cheese are a part of the Chinese diet; the decadent Western influence on Hong Kong has, however, brought in these great innovations. Actually, of over a billion people in China, at any one time over 200 million are squatting down by a cutting board, chopping things up to go into the pot for lunch or dinner.

I look on the sandwich not only as a great time saver, but also as an opportunity to be creative. It may, however, be possible to be *too* creative. Our friend Ebberline used to make a sandwich this way: He'd take a jar of goose grease that his mother had saved from their Thanksgiving goose out of the refrigerator, spread a thick layer of it on a piece of bread, and then slice radishes into the goo. Presto—a radish sandwich. I can't say I ever tried it myself; maybe it was good.

I'm more of a traditionalist. Give me pastrami on rye. Make sure that the pastrami you buy is sliced very thin. Then sort of fold it back and forth on the bread, rather than laying it down in neat layers; the folded piles make it look bigger and more magnificent. Then add horseradish mustard, one of the sublime creations of the age. (You'll find it easier to spread the mustard on the bread rather than on the meat.) A cultural note: The summer I taught in Montreal, I learned that there they call pastrami "smoked meat." So, if you're ever in Montreal and you want pastrami, ask for smoked meat. It's a big thing there, and the stuff they have is excellent.

This same principle of folding the meat back and forth applies, of course, to other kinds of meat, such as corned beef, roast beef, or ham. The thinner the slice, the better. I learned this from a deli owner in Baltimore: thin meat, fluffed up and folded back and forth. It makes for a more tender and flavorful mouthful. This is particularly applicable if your choppers aren't as sharp as they used to be. It's a drag trying to gnaw through a thick piece of roast beef or ham, especially if you pull the meat out of the sandwich with your teeth: You're sitting there with half a sandwich hanging out of your mouth and mayonnaise dripping down your new tie. The thin-slice/folding practice is what makes the Arby's roast beef sandwich such a success.

Slicing things thin is an art that takes considerable practice. Nine Fingers Naguchi, the sushi chef, got sent to the farm club in Billings, Montana, because he couldn't slice the fish thin enough. Unless you want to go to the trouble of buying a meat slicer like they have at the deli counter (they're a bitch to clean), you'll have to content yourself with either buying all your lunch meat presliced or learning how to make a thin slice. Since leftover ham and roast beef are true naturals for sandwiches, you'll just have to perfect your technique: Get a really good, sharp knife and work on it. I've been using a serrated blade that's one of the most wonderful gifts I've ever received. An electric knife works pretty well, too. Just be careful where you place your thumb; it might end up in the sandwich and spoil your whole day. Proper wrist action and a good eye are prerequisites for the thin slice. Practice on an onion.

▸ SELECTING THE BREAD

A lot of people pay great attention to what goes into a sandwich and forget that good bread is one of the real fundamentals for success. I think that eating white bread is like eating air: There's just not much to it. If you really want to make your sandwich an affirmation of blandness, put it on store-bought white bread. The bakery I used to work at put out a pretty substantial loaf of white bread. If you can't find good bakery bread, you're probably not trying very hard, but an acceptable alternative is Pepperidge Farm. I like the good crust on it.

I'm not sure why Americans have such a thing for spongy-soft white bread. I once saw a hausfrau in Omaha go right down the bread aisle, squeezing each of the loaves of white bread, leaving a massive thumbprint in each, in quest of the freshest one. She obviously didn't realize that they'd all gotten off the truck in the same load; about all that you could say for them was that they were fresh. The poor silly woman thought she was being a conscientious shopper. She no doubt brought home a loaf that had the consistency of cotton candy and then ripped right through it as she slathered on peanut butter for the assembled urchins.

My friend Leo spent the last year of World War II in Belgium hiding out from the Nazi draft officer (he was sixteen at the time). He told me that an American soldier gave him a piece of white bread, which he'd not seen in six years, and he put it in his shirt and ran home several miles to share it with his brother and sisters. Even Leo, despite his experience, isn't too keen on white bread.

It's a mystery to me why so much white bread is sold in this country. Look at the bread shelf in the supermarket. There are *yards* of the stuff. One summer during undergraduate years, I was a gas jockey at one of the stops along the Illinois Tollway, and three boys from Austria were among my fellow workers. They just couldn't stand the white bread. It took some little time of experimentation before they found something with enough substance to please them. They also had a hard time with those little cans of hot dogs that are laughingly called Vienna sausages. Truth in packaging be damned. They thought America was a great place; they were just a bit mystified over some of the things we did. One asked me once why it was that people here thought they were from Australia. Beats me. On the other hand, I knew a woman from Maryland who thought that Nebraska was somewhere near Idaho. I suppose no place has a patent on ignorance. I've since visited Austria, and people there aren't too sure where Nebraska is, either. The bread in Austria, by the way, is excellent, as is the beer.

One additional thought on why Americans eat white bread: conformity. Everybody grew up on this glop, so breaking away from the pattern is a difficult thing to do. Conformity is a powerful force. Judy and I were sitting on the porch one time and saw three little girls, each maybe about ten years old, walking down the sidewalk. Two were barefoot, carrying their shoes; the third we couldn't see because she was behind a car. Judy wondered if she was carrying *her* shoes, too, and I allowed as how there was no force on earth that could keep shoes on that child's feet right then. She came around the car and, sure enough. We can blame all of this on the pernicious influence of white bread. It may build strong bodies twelve ways, but it turns your brain to mud.

My theory is the darker the better when it comes to bread. You don't have to be Jewish to love Levy's. Give me black rye; give me a kaiser roll, give me some pumpernickel. We get some wonderful Italian hard rolls in Omaha that are perfect for a substantial sandwich; they're especially good with Italian sausage and sweet peppers, where you need a good thick crust to keep the insides from leaking through the bread. Shop around until you find the kind of bread you like, and try several in different applications. I'm a sucker for whole wheat toast and for rye bread in a meat sandwich. You'll want white or whole wheat for grilled cheese or tuna sandwiches; rye just isn't right for these. A tip: If you've got several loaves of bread going at the same time, forget about a bread box; put them in the refrigerator to keep them from drying out or getting moldy.

Toasting does wonders for bread, but be sure not to get it too dark; you'll lose the flavor of the bread. This goes for rolls and hamburger buns as well. No, don't try to wedge them into the toaster; lay the halves out inside-up on a cookie sheet and put them into your broiler for a minute or less. It puts a nice crunchy surface on the inside of the bun and gives it some character. Try a little butter and garlic powder on it before you toast and you'll have some real zip.

▸ THE BLT

Bacon, lettuce, and tomato on whole wheat toast is wonderful. It's wonderful, at least, if you have some real tomatoes, not the green rocks that they strip-mine in Texas. I grow my own, so I at least get the taste of a real tomato three months out of each year. A few pointers: Put the mayonnaise on *both* pieces of toast, so you can get enough of it on there to give some taste. Be generous with the bacon and cheap with the lettuce. Slice the tomato thin.

Judy *loves* the BLT, and a point of compatibility in our marriage is that we share the same opinion of those grainy tomatoes from the store. They *gas* them to turn them red. We revel in homegrown tomatoes come July. Bob, our older son, is in essential agreement with this family policy. Pete, on the other hand, is firmly against tomatoes of all kinds and makes no bones about it. We've been wondering where we went wrong. I have suggested that Pete may be a Communist, as he won't eat peanut butter, either, which is un-American. He will, however, eat fish. His older brother regards this with horror. But I digress. More sandwiches:

▸ GRILLED CHEESE

I like Velveeta in a grilled-cheese sandwich, but try whatever turns you on. I can't imagine Cheddar in a grilled-cheese sandwich, but somebody might like it. Every cripple dances his own way. On the other hand, Monterey Jack might make for a very interesting sandwich. I use a wire cheese cutter, which works much better than a knife; it's got a thin wire stretched tighter than the E string on a cheap guitar from Sears. It just glides through that cheese and doesn't stick to it like a knife would. Forget the presliced cheese in the plastic wrap; you're paying mostly for plastic; also, it's troublesome to unwrap the plastic from each slice of cheese, and they're too thin to be of much use. The secret to a good grilled cheese is to get the butter or margarine on the outside pieces uniformly.

Try this: Slightly melt margarine in the microwave, about twenty seconds per quarter-pound stick, and proportionately less for smaller pieces. Go easy and experiment with this—you don't want it in a puddle, just soft enough to spread without putting it through the bread. Lay your first buttered bread down on the griddle and then assemble the sandwich. Two strips of bacon or a thin slice of ham gives a grilled-cheese sandwich some substance. After laying on the cheese, put the top piece of buttered bread on. Getting your action right for the flip and knowing when to flip are things you'll have to learn by experience.

▸ THE REUBEN

I wouldn't go to the trouble of making Reubens for myself; however, if you're entertaining, they make a hit. I just looked *Reuben* up in the dictionary to get the inventor's first name (Arnold Reuben, 1883–1970), and it says the sandwich contains Swiss cheese, turkey, ham, coleslaw, and Russian dressing. They've got it all wrong, although that sounds like an interesting sandwich. Try it if you like. To me, a Reuben contains corned beef, sauerkraut, and either Monterey Jack or Swiss cheese, prepared on the grill the same way you'd do a grilled cheese, only in this case using rye bread. Go heavy on the corned beef and cheese, light on the sauerkraut. I don't know where they came up with the idea of Russian dressing and coleslaw; sounds weird. Some like to add a little Thousand Island dressing.

▸ TUNA

Tuna fish, I think, is just great. I had some raw tuna at a sushi bar one time and was surprised to find out that it didn't taste like fish. Perhaps all that Kirin beer had blunted my taste buds. Just about any kind of canned tuna is acceptable—the generic kind is just as good as the most expensive. Just be sure to get *chunk* style, not grated. Grated tuna is fit for cats, but not for humans. I prefer the oil-packed to the water-packed. In either case, be sure to take the lid off the can all the way around and then use it to press in on the tuna to squeeze the fluid out of the can; otherwise, you'll have a mess of wet fish. Fork it out into a bowl, breaking up the chunks as you go. Add two tablespoons of Miracle Whip, which to me has more flavor than regular mayonnaise, and stir it all up. There are several optional ingredients that give this basic tuna-mayonnaise mix some character; add one or more as you like it: a tablespoon or more of catsup helps things out, a tablespoon of piccalilli or some finely chopped sweet pickles, about a tablespoon of chopped onion or an equal amount of chopped celery, or all of the above. I have a friend who also adds one or more chopped hard-boiled eggs, which I think is a good thing if you have only one can of tuna to feed six people and you're trying to stretch things. Spread the mix thickly on the bread. For a different approach, grill your tuna fish sandwich the same way you would a grilled cheese.

You can make chicken salad pretty much the same

way you make tuna salad: mayonnaise, onion, celery, pickle, a little catsup. I guess I don't know anyone who'd actually like to make chicken salad. The same goes for egg salad. If I were making egg salad, I'd include all of the above and then throw in a can of tuna and make it tuna salad.

This goes a little beyond sandwiches, but I make a dandy shrimp and lobster salad using these same basic ingredients: boiled eggs, chopped onion, sweet pickle relish, chopped celery, Miracle Whip, and catsup, all in generous proportions. Our local supermarket sells live lobsters, which are too expensive for this kind of proposition, but when it looks like they're about to die of natural causes, they boil them up and sell them at the deli counter for four bucks a piece. This meat is plenty good enough to go into a salad, and you don't have to mess with boiling the lobsters. I stretch it with some shrimp, about a pound of the small ones. Boil the shrimp for about four minutes and then get them into cold water right away; don't let the shrimp sit around in the boiling water, as overcooked shrimp are at first tough and then start to deteriorate. You might even keep some in the refrigerator while you're peeling the first batch. Shrimp-lobster salad is always a real hit, and it's as easy as tuna salad: Just blend the meat with the other stuff I've listed, keep it cold until you serve it, and serve a glob of it on a lettuce leaf. Good eating.

▸ FRANKFURTERS

There isn't much to cooking a hot dog, but our friend Linda is able to screw it up, so I thought I'd better comment before going on to greater things. She puts the weenie in the bun and then microwaves the whole thing. I suppose this is all right at one of those automated lunch counters where you get a plastic bag full of hot dog out of a machine, but it just doesn't cut it as far as I'm concerned. For starters, microwaving bread makes it tough without putting a crust on it. If you want warm bread, better to broil it or even put it facedown on the grill for a moment; that will put a crust on it without toughening the bread itself. In fact, it makes a stale bun more tender. The other problem with microwaving a hot dog in the bun is that the grease from the frank goes right into the bun. At the very least, boil your hot dogs for a minute or two, so that the excess grease melts out into the water. If you've gone to the trouble of buying a truly noble hot dog, though, grill it. I've not tried turkey hot dogs, and I don't intend to. I like Wranglers and Hygrade's Ball Park franks. They're nice and fat, not like these little ten for seventy-nine cents weenies you'd feed your kids' friends. Get some hot dogs that have some substance and cook them on the charcoal grill, being careful not to put a black crust on the meat. If you live in an absurd climate like I do, where you can only peer at the grill outside among the drifts, split the hot dogs down the middle and grill them on the stove. The split frank makes a nice trough to load up the piccalilli and chopped onion, kraut, or leftover chili. I buy my kraut in a small can, just heat up what my son Bob and I will eat (we live with two other people who are antikraut as a matter of policy), and throw away the rest. Is it a sin to throw away food? No, not as much of a sin as it is to leave a half bowl of used sauerkraut lying around in the refrigerator. This can cause more domestic strife than habitually leaving the toilet seat up. Saving a dime's worth of kraut isn't worth the hassle.

A nice alternative way of preparing frankfurters is with bacon and cheese. Fry the bacon the way you usually would but arrest the process about three-quarters of the way through, just before it starts to get crusty. Drain it on some paper towels. Split the hot dogs down the middle, being careful not to cut all the way through. Lay strips of your favorite cheese down the splits and then wrap each of the franks with a strip of bacon; line them up on a cookie sheet and broil them in the oven until the cheese starts to melt. Serve by themselves or on buns. If you're serving them without buns, it's handy to pin the bacon onto the hot dog with a toothpick. This is only for the fastidious. Judy and I lived on this when we were first married. (This and her Swiss steak, which is one of the reasons I ultimately agreed to take over the cooking.) Sweet corn was a staple, too. Judy had just graduated from nursing school, and I was still an undergraduate. We rented the top part of a farmhouse outside of De Kalb, Illinois; sixty dollars per month. On a hot, still day, it's possible to lie there and actually *hear* the corn grow. No kidding. I took a part-time job for a while in a bakery, and she was concerned that I wasn't being supported in a proper manner, bless her heart. In addition to frankfurters, we saw a lot of three-pounds-for-a-dollar hamburger from the Piggly Wiggly. Well, this is *déjà vu* all over again.

Cut-up hot dogs are an obvious plus for baked beans, chili, or German potato salad. Boil them a little first to get the grease out. My friend O'Reilly used to go with a girl who swore that at her private girls' school they never served whole hot dogs, only ones that had been chopped up. We were mystified, but she said that they also sharpened the mop and broom handle ends to a point. This seems a bit thick to me, but I suppose one can't be too careful. I have it on good authority, however, that a hot dog makes for a less than substantial dildo. I should think that a cucumber would provide more of what's wanted. On the same theme, I once saw a stripper in Denver do the boiled-egg trick, which was a real crowd pleaser. Placing your food into places upon your person other than your mouth, however, goes beyond the scope of this book.

Canned chili is plenty good enough for chili dogs, which are a good thing to eat if you're wearing an old shirt and you don't mind what gets on it. People get persnickety about their chili, a topic that we'll treat at greater length later on. I don't find the canned stuff to be too bad, though, especially if you're going to put it on frankfurters. Just remember that a little goes a long, long way.

▸ FRENCH DIP

There's no mystery at all to the French-dip sandwich, which is just a roast beef sandwich on a hard roll with some beef bouillon to dip it into. I presume that the name derives from the fact that the sandwich is usually on French bread and that one dips it, and that it's not a commentary on the individual who invented the sandwich. Again, here is an example of a sandwich with quality that is directly proportional to the thinness of the meat and the crustiness of the bread. Presumably you can find a good source of French bread. I would split and broil it a bit, not only to bring out the flakiness of the crust but also to add a crusty edge to the inside. Getting your beef thin enough, though, is the key. There are those who despair of ever getting the hang of slicing meat thinly, or who won't even try. My father, in his usual haste, would lop off hunks of a roast that were about a half-inch thick. Such leftover slabs are no good for a French dip, which should have delicate, wafer-thin slices piled high. Most good deli counters sell already roasted beef and have the counter attendant *shave* the meat on the slicing machine.

This goes for ham, also. Meat-counter attendants, as well, aim to please. If slicing meat is more trouble than it's worth for you, have the butcher slice your ham for you when you buy it; there's no extra charge. Finally, the bouillon for dipping should be strong. Fortunately they're now selling bouillon crystals, which dissolve much better than the old bouillon cubes.

▸ BARBECUED BEEF

There are several variations on the barbecued-meat sandwich, and there are almost as many people who are willing to be a pain in the ass about barbecue as there are connoisseurs of chili. If you're such a person, you've already got your barbecue recipe figured out; go on to the next section. Let's continue, though, with the basic assumption that is behind this book: Most men don't know how to cook, and the primary thing that most mothers taught their sons was guilt. Now on to a simple, slapdash method of doing barbecue beef—or pork or lamb or mystery meat—sandwiches that doesn't take four hours. The leftover slabs from one of my father's roasts are perfect for barbecued beef. Slice up these hunks of meat into pieces fairly thin (perhaps a quarter of an inch) and long (about an inch to an inch and a half). You want small pieces of meat in a sandwich so that it will be tender. You'll want to put the finished product on something more substantial than white bread unless you enjoy having your sandwich dissolve in your hands. A kaiser roll or French bread would be perfect, but a hamburger bun toasted on the inside will do. Now here's how to go about it: Dice some onion, about a third of a fair-sized one, and sauté it in a little oil until the edges of the onion pieces are starting to brown. Add the sliced beef and stir-fry on fairly high heat for a few minutes until the beef (or other meat) starts to brown a little also. We're assuming that you're using leftover meat that's already been cooked, so don't go overboard and cook it too much more here. If you've got a nice mess of meat, say, two cups or so, the additional frying shouldn't take much more than five minutes. Add about two tablespoons of brown sugar, turn down the heat to medium-low, and pour regular white vinegar over the brown sugar, about two or three tablespoons. Enjoy the aroma as the vinegar starts to boil. Toss in some catsup, perhaps three or four tablespoons (as you can tell, I usually don't measure; I just dump it in until it seems like enough; I'll be damned if I'm going to stand there with a tablespoon measuring catsup) and about half as much mustard. Salt and pepper to taste as you stir it all together. Heat just until the whole concoction is warmed and spoon it out onto your toasted buns. Beauty. This is the one spicy thing I remember from childhood, and I was so used to blandness coming out of Mother's kitchen that it took me some little time to figure out that barbecue was good to eat. My mother is actually a hell of a cook, but Pop had indigestion on a more or less permanent basis (probably more as a result of his job than anything else), so she went easy on the spicy stuff. I seem to remember a regular offering of warmed-over roast beef slices swimming in brown gravy; I try to avoid that sort of thing myself. If you've got leftover meat, use this tried-and-true method for making barbecue.

The same system goes for sloppy joes. The only difference is that with a sloppy joe you're starting with fresh hamburger instead of leftover roast beef. Break up the hamburger with your fingers as you drop it into the frying pan; the more you crumble it as it goes in, the less work you'll have as it cooks. Brown it over medium-high heat, stirring and turning it to get it evenly cooked. Cook it until it's past the color gray and approaching brown. Now push the meat over to the side of your pan with the spatula and tilt the pan so that the hamburger grease collects in a puddle on the side. I tried for years to pour this grease off without dumping out the crumbled, browned hamburger, with varying degrees of success. Our friend Rosalie taught me how to get this done more quickly and easily without pouring either hot grease or cooked hamburger all over the kitchen counter. Use a turkey baster, one of those big eyedroppers that looks like something you'd test antifreeze with, to suck the grease out of the pan and into your empty bean can. This is one of the tricks of the trade that is worth the price of the book itself, and I didn't learn it myself until five years ago; it's astonishingly simple and efficient.

Perhaps this trick is nothing new to you, but I stood there slackjawed in awe when I first saw it, kind of like the cavemen in *Quest for Fire* when Rae Dawn Chong started rubbing sticks together. Why didn't I think of that? Because of the power of association, I now murmur, "God bless Rosalie Jorgensen," every time I use a turkey baster to suck grease out of a pan. I have some other associations relating to food. For example, I always think of Dean Rusk when I'm pouring orange juice. The origin of that one is lost in the mists of memory.

Once you've got a frying pan full of cooked hamburger and onion, the sloppy joes are assembled just the same way as we've already done barbecued beef: brown sugar, vinegar, catsup, mustard, salt, and pepper. You might need to toss in a little more catsup to get the color right. Then heat it up good and ladle it out onto toasted buns. A point: If you've gone overboard on the vinegar and catsup, this stuff will still be in too liquid a form to use for sandwiches. Cook it for another five or ten minutes (without a lid), and some of the fluid will evaporate off, making your sloppy joes less sloppy.

▸ THE HAMBURGER

If you've cooked at all, you've probably cooked hamburgers, so we won't need to spend much time on them. I like to beat mine out thin and big around; they cook faster that way than if they're in thick little lumps. They're best on the grill, but whatever way you cook them, use high heat to brown the outside without drying out the inside. I've tried various ways of jazzing up hamburgers, including onion soup mix in with the ground meat and various other adulterants, and I still go back to the basic hamburger on a toasted bun with a slice of raw onion. I'll throw on a slice of cheese every now and then, just before the hamburgers are quite cooked, but I've gotten away from trying different kinds of chefs' blends to disguise the simple, honest hamburger. Better to put it on a different kind of bread than to mess with hamburgers the way God intended them to be. An onion roll, again, slightly toasted on the inside, makes an elegant platform for a hamburger. Dark rye makes for a more exotic approach. In Baltimore, they line up several small hamburgers on a long French roll with grilled onions. Lovely.

There's a certain *sociableness* to the hamburger, the centerpiece of the great American cookout. The smell of burning flesh, mosquito repellent on hairy legs, deviled eggs with ants. It kind of chokes you up, doesn't it? George Bullock saved his political hide with hamburgers once. George, an implement dealer in Athens, Georgia, was chairman of the Clarke County Commission. My one fling with elective office was a term on the Clarke County Democratic Committee. George was chair of that, too. The issue was this: Being the smallest county in the state of Georgia, it seemed to many of us that there would be certain economies to be realized if city government in Athens and county government in Clarke County could be consolidated. George was against this, of course, as it would put him out of a job as a county commissioner. When consolidation came to a vote, and this was maybe fifteen years ago now, George took it upon himself to write a letter against it, which was published in the town paper. He couldn't use county letterhead, since the commissioners were on record as favoring consolidation. So he wrote the letter to the paper on Clarke County Democratic Committee letterhead, thus implying that party leadership (and there just *were* no Republicans in Georgia that year) was against consolidating city and county government. We'd not, however, taken a position on the issue as a group, but most of us as individuals were very much in favor of it. The membership was hopping mad.

Now, you're wondering what all this has to do with hamburgers, right? Hang on, we're getting to that.

George, the old fox, knew that he was in deep shit. So what did he do? I'll tell you what he did. He called the next regularly scheduled meeting to be at his lake house, and he treated us to delicious hamburgers, beer, and all the associated goodies. We went through the motions of voting to censure him, but it was halfhearted and lost by a couple of votes. You just can't kick a guy's ass while you're eating his hamburgers and drinking his beer. Remember this the next time they're coming for you with torches and pitchforks.

▸ THE HERO SANDWICH

Call it the hoagie, the submarine, or the hero, it's pretty much the same thing with a few regional variations. The basic place to start is with the bread, a hoagie roll that looks something like a partially deflated football. In Omaha we tend to use Italian rolls with a hard, chewy crust. French bread is also good. The essential idea of the sandwich is a nice, long piece of crusty bread loaded with salami, ham, cheese, whatever turns you on. Pastrami, which one usually associates with dark rye, adds vigor to a hero sandwich. I'm frankly pro-pastrami, and I make no bones about it. Grilled Polish sausage goes good in a hoagie bun. An interesting variation I've seen on the usual hero sandwich of meat and cheese adds shredded lettuce, with vinegar and oil sprinkled over the lettuce and topped off with a dusting of oregano. Be sure to use the flaked oregano rather than the powdered kind. It gives the sandwich a nice twist. Bob and I took a couple of these to an all-night science fiction movie festival and broke them out about four in the morning. We were surrounded there in the dark by envious sobs as the smell of the salami and vinegar permeated the theater. Shaved ham and Swiss cheese make for another wonderful hero, especially if it's topped off with that blessing to mankind, horseradish mustard.

There are few things one can trust any more. Marriages are falling apart all around us; kids are suing their parents because they grew up to be assholes. Grandparents are shacking up. The government sucks. Horseradish mustard is one of the few verities left to us, something that we can really depend upon. Others find truth and beauty in more fundamental kinds of food; I'll stick with spicy brown mustard.

I once sat across the lunch table from a dear old thing in our church, Goldie, who was eighty-nine at the time. Goldie has now gone on to her reward, but she left me with a bit of wisdom. I asked her, "Goldie, what has really given you strength during your long life? What can you really depend on?"

She looked at me for a thoughtful minute and then replied, with perfect sincerity, "Taters."

"I beg your pardon?"

"Taters. I like them mashed, boiled, and fried. When my man was alive, we had taters two, three times a day."

Here was a woman who had built a long, honest life around the common potato. How can one argue with her?

▸ LOX AND BAGELS

Others may find strength and sustenance in more exotic things, but I nominate the lox-and-bagel sandwich as an example of true nobility in the sandwich universe. I wind up buying Nova Scotia lox by the slice, rather than by the pound, because I live on a professor's salary. The woman at the deli counter understands. Fortunately, a little lox goes a long way. I like onion bagels, split and buttered, then broiled until there's a light brown crust on the inside of the bagel. Then slatherings of cream cheese, topped off with a couple of slices of lox. (One can buy refrigerated sliced, smoked salmon even in those less civilized areas where you can't find a good deli counter. I was forced to learn this when we lived in Athens, Georgia, where an ethnic restaurant is a Pizza Hut.)

I was shocked to find that good Jewish food is not available in Israel. They served us beautiful lox and bagels on the El Al flight from JFK to Tel Aviv, but then we were subjected to two weary weeks of boiled beef. It was explained to me that one doesn't go to Israel for the food. That's an understatement. We were so sick of the hotel food after a while that we went searching for something with flavor. Finally, we found a Chinese restaurant near the King David Hotel in Jerusalem, and we had some good old American sweet and sour pork. A feast! I asked the waiter if it was kosher, and he laughed, "Sure. We've got a Chinese rabbi in the kitchen."

El Al rates high in my book in terms of airline food, much of which on other airlines is pretty dismal. Japan Airlines is also quite good. I had a meal on Continental not too long ago; it was no better than I deserved. The most miserable meal I ever had on a plane was on a flight from Atlanta to Houston, and it wasn't the airline's fault. The plane was packed full and the young woman next to me was forced to hold her toddler in her lap, except for the three or four times the kid had to get up and pee. I was sympathetic, having been through this routine with my own kids many times before. The young momma was in the window seat, of course; I was in the middle, and on the outside was a woman who had formerly served as a matron at the Black Hole of Calcutta. It was pretty grim. By the time Eastern served their celebrated casserole of cactus and rocks, we were ready for food in any form, having spent the usual two hours on the ground in Atlanta. There was, however, just no way this poor thing was going to handle both the baby and the fold-down dinner tray. Inspired, I volunteered to shovel down my dinner quickly—which was the only way you could handle eating this stuff anyway—and then take a turn with the kid while Little Momma got fed. Silly me.

Now, you can get away with plopping a six-month-old into a stranger's lap for the few minutes it takes to inhale food that has neither texture nor taste. The kid will play with your buttons or pull your mustache, and you'll generally get along all right. You can't get away with that, however, with the average, intelligent twenty-two-month-old. This kid had a finely honed sense of territoriality and set up a howl that the pilot could hear, forty-eight rows in front of us. Mom wasn't foolish enough, of course, to give up her one and only chance at sustenance, bad as it was. And even though the little girl was less than six inches away from her mommy, you'd have thought she was being spirited away by storm troopers. The hearing in my left ear is still a little off. Baby looked desperately over at Mom and thrashed about while I tried to hold her down and keep her from kicking or clawing Battle-ax on the other side of me, who would have eaten her whole and spit out the seed. Little Snookims was, of course, all happy and smiles when we got off and her grandparents were there to meet her. The person meeting me—for a job interview, as it happens—must have thought that I'd just stepped out of a Waring blender.

▸ SOUPS AND SALADS

To me, the sandwich is the basic foundation of a good lunch; throw in a few potato chips along with a good sandwich or two and I'm happy. If you're really going to spread yourself, though, have something in addition to sandwiches. Either soup or salad, or both, make for a complete meal.

Any idiot can make a tossed green salad. I'm fascinated, though, at the trouble people can go to in the preparation of a salad. Judy rips the lettuce all apart, washes it, runs it through a plastic centrifuge that she bought at some house party ("What in the hell is that?" "It's a lettuce dryer"), and then *lays it out to dry* on a dish towel because the lettuce dryer doesn't work very well. Thus, a simple lettuce salad takes her about half an hour to prepare.

Now, I personally have never seen a dirty head of lettuce. I think they must hose them off in the store before chucking them into the cellophane bags. I don't see much reason to wash lettuce unless there's obvious soil on the outside of it; then just rinse off the outside, not every damn leaf. The plant itself provides protection to the inside leaves and keeps them from getting dirty. Further, the kind of washing one would give a head of lettuce would just knock off some of the dirt, not really get anything *clean.* Are you nuts about cleanliness? Do you take three showers a day and spray the telephone receiver with Lysol? Then take each lettuce leaf and scrub it down with hot water and Comet cleanser. Talk about taking the joy out of life.

Everybody says that you must *tear* your lettuce, not cut it with a knife. Why the hell not? Go ahead and cut the lettuce any way you want. One note, though: Use a clean knife. A food-science professor once pointed out to me that a dandy way to spread food poisoning is to cut lettuce with the same knife you've used to cut up a chicken. (Raw chicken, by the way, is particularly filthy; be careful to wash both your knife and your cutting board after you've cut up a chicken.) Another note: Getting the stem or core out of the head of lettuce is easy; just slam the head down on the counter directly on the stem, and it will lift right out.

Rip, tear, or cut up the lettuce into a bowl and then add whatever you like for a tossed salad. Spinach, maybe (you will have to wash the spinach; they rub sand on it as it leaves the factory), or radishes, chopped celery, cucumber, Bermuda onion, green pepper, tomatoes, any of the stuff you've seen at a salad bar that turns you on. I like to put bacon chips (the real ones, not the ones made out of soybean meal), coarse black pepper, and grated Parmesan cheese over a salad. There are any number of fine salad dressings for sale at the store, so I can't see going to great lengths to make salad dressing. Do you want a chef's salad? Just throw some strips of ham and cheese, maybe some boiled egg, and a couple of olives on top, and you've got chef's salad.

▸ FRUIT SALAD

A good fruit salad is better than tossed green salad and even easier to prepare. Just cut up a bunch of fruit into a bowl and mix it together. Forget about dressing for a fruit salad; there'll be enough fruit juice swapping around loose to dress it just fine. A few tips: If you're going to have fresh peaches in your salad, look out that they don't turn brown on you. Either sprinkle a little lemon juice over them after they're sliced and mix them up in it or slice some oranges in with the peach slices and stir them together. The citrus keeps the peaches from browning. I like sliced bananas, white grapes, strawberries, bing cherries, melon, apples, oranges, and peaches all together in a fruit salad. Maybe some fresh pineapple if you can get it.

Perhaps as a holdover from my years in Georgia, I am a grower of peaches. There's a certain disadvantage to living in Nebraska and raising peaches. Nothing against Nebraska—the folks here can raise corn with the best of them—but there are very few other peach growers in this part of the country. It could be, of course, that they know something.

The trees themselves I get on mail order from the Gurney Company, an outfit in Yankton, South Dakota, that raises really hearty trees. Therefore the cold winters here don't kill the trees themselves. However, every other year we get a late frost that knocks out the peach blossoms. So I'm really excited when we *do* get a crop. When my trees were younger and had first flowered, a cold snap came on, and I was running around like a madman covering the trees with blankets and sheets. Judy said I looked like I was trying to save my children. The trees are too big for that now, so I just have to hope and pray, and we tough it out together.

47•LUNCH

The Gurney Company publishes a seed catalog for true believers. After five months of winter, I pore over the thing and believe everything it says. I, too, can grow beautiful, colossal vegetables. They really *will* be as green and juicy as the ones in the pictures. The center spread is the best part of the seed catalog: down-home news items with pictures of kids standing next to prizewinning pumpkins. Folk wisdom from the heartland, people who have cellars full of tomatoes they've put up in mason jars. I sent in a picture one time of a gigantic peace rose I'd grown from a Gurney rosebush, and they published it in the center spread and sent me a check for seven dollars. *Professional photographer.*

Trying to regain that rush, that kind of peak experience, has been a goal of mine in the years since. I now know how the star halfback on the high school football team feels; everything left in life is an anticlimax. He'll never have that much attention given to him again as long as he lives. I've sent in pictures of other roses, of prize crookneck squash, buckets of beans, peach tree branches that have to be propped up because of the weight of the fruit.

No dice.

I'm working on a strategy now to get back into the Gurney seed catalog center spread. They seem to like to print pictures of little kids looking cute as they stand next to the bounty grown from Gurney seed and plants. The problem is that my younger son, Pete, is fifteen and pushing six feet. He left "cute" behind somewhere in the third grade. But I have a plan: I have this dwarf cherry tree that is just loaded, and all the cherries are turning red at the same time. I've been posing Pete standing with his knees in a pair of my old shoes. From the right angle, damned if he doesn't look like a dwarf. Maybe a stretch version, but a dwarf nonetheless. I figure that the Gurney people will go for a picture of a dwarf kid standing next to a dwarf tree. I'll make sure that Pete shaves really well, and we'll sort of hide some of the top half of him in the lower branches. It's worth a try.

▸ COLESLAW

Coleslaw is a lot of trouble, and nine times out of ten I just buy a quart of it at the deli counter and get along that way. If you're compulsive, though, and have to make your own, here's how: Wash a head of cabbage, then slice it thin; chop up the slices. Put it into a big bowl. In a separate bowl, mix up a couple of tablespoons of sour cream, the same amount of Miracle Whip, a tablespoon of lemon juice, a tablespoon of sugar, a teaspoon of salt, maybe a teaspoon of prepared horseradish if you like coleslaw with some zip, and blend in enough vinegar to make a smooth mixture that's fairly runny. Pour this sauce over the chopped cabbage and mix it all up. For variety, add a couple of grated carrots, or use half red cabbage and half green.

▸ JELL-O

Jell-O makes for a passable salad; but don't start whipping up some Jell-O when you're running late, because it takes some time to firm up as it cools. Just follow the directions on the package. Make sure the powder all gets dissolved in the first cup of hot water. To speed the cooling process, you can include ice cubes in the second cup of water, which is supposed to be cold. Then, pop it into the refrigerator and let it harden up. Be sure to use the exact measurements for water that are prescribed on the box; Jell-O with too little water is rubbery. As the gelatin is starting to thicken up, toss in some fruit: pineapple chunks, sliced bananas, cherries, orange slices, anything to give the Jell-O some interest. You don't want to put the fruit in too soon or it won't stay in the middle of the Jell-O. Wait until it's thickened up to the consistency of honey, stir in your fruit, and put it back into the cooler until it gets firm. For a change, substitute a cup of ginger ale for the water.

A point of information: Don't use fresh pineapple in your Jell-O or it will never firm up. It has to do with the enzymes in the fresh pineapple preventing the rubberization process. My mother told me about this, and I didn't believe her. I tried it twice and had Jell-O soup both times. Nothing could be done to salvage it, either. *Canned* pineapple chunks work just fine. A boy should always listen to his mother.

▸ POTATO SALAD

Potato salad goes well with lots of things, especially hamburgers, hot dogs, or ham. There are two distinct kinds of potato salad; we'll cover both. For regular potato salad, peel about four big or six medium-size potatoes and boil them. My mother peels them after they're boiled; I don't like having to mess with hot potatoes, so I peel mine first. There's an art to getting them cooked just right; you want them firm and not mushy. Boil for about fifteen or twenty minutes and stick them with a fork to see how they're doing. Potatoes that are cut into quarters cook a little faster. At the point when they're soft when you stick in the fork, pour off the boiling water and cool them with cold water but don't let them sit around in it. Better to just pour off the cold water and let them finish cooling on the countertop. In the meantime, hard-boil six eggs and chop up about a cup of celery, one good-size green pepper, and a medium-size onion. In a separate bowl, combine four or five tablespoons of mayonnaise, a tablespoon of sugar, a teaspoon of salt, two tablespoons of mustard, and a couple of tablespoons of vinegar. Cut up the potatoes into pieces about half an inch square, and mix them together with the onion, celery, green pepper, and five of the cooked eggs that have been chopped up. Add the other stuff along with three tablespoons of sweet pickle relish and toss it with two big spoons until it's all mixed up. Add more mayonnaise if it's still too dry. After you've mixed it to your satisfaction, slice the last boiled egg over the top. Refrigerate and serve cold.

▸ GERMAN POTATO SALAD

Cook up your potatoes the same way as for regular potato salad and chop them up about the same size. In the meantime, fry six or eight pieces of bacon until crisp; drain the bacon on paper towel, but save the bacon grease—pour it into a small saucepan. Add eight tablespoons of cider vinegar to the bacon grease, a half cup of diced onion, a teaspoon of salt, and a half teaspoon of paprika; warm it on the stove but don't cook it too long. Then, in a large bowl, combine the cooked potatoes and the stuff you've cooked in the saucepan, tossing it lightly to combine without mushing up the potatoes, adding the crumbled-up bacon as you go. Mix thoroughly.This stuff should be served hot. If you can't serve it immediately, you can keep it warm in a large, covered saucepan on *very* low heat, stirring it occasionally. I usually don't get too excited about salads, and I suspect that most men agree with me, but this stuff has some substance, and it's good as a side dish with lots of things. Try it with grilled sausage and kraut and lots of cold beer. It's nice with baked ham as well, or many different meat dishes.

▸ TUNA-MACARONI SALAD

This stuff is good to serve with cheese and cold cuts and a big pitcher of iced tea on one of those days in August when nobody wants to eat anything hot. Boil up a cup of elbow macaroni, following the label directions; pour it out into a colander (that's the big bowl with holes in it and little feet) to drain and rinse it with cold water; let the cold water drain off. Fix tuna salad the way we've already described, but add half a cup of bottled French salad dressing and go heavy on the chopped celery and onion. Mix the tuna salad with the cooled macaroni and add two tablespoons of lemon juice (in almost all cases where we call for lemon juice, Realemon is perfectly acceptable; don't be wasting your time squeezing fresh lemons). Refrigerate until well chilled, at least two hours, and serve a nice big glob of it on a lettuce leaf. This makes for an acceptable alternative to regular-style potato salad, and it's much easier to prepare. This stuff will keep for several days in a tightly sealed container, but, as with all things having a mayonnaise base, be sure to keep it refrigerated and don't leave the bowl out too long in the heat.

▸ WALDORF SALAD

I doubt that this is what they're serving at the Waldorf this year, but here's the way I go about it: Cut up about five nice apples; you don't have to peel them, but do get rid of the cores. Slice them thin, getting about twenty to twenty-four slices out of each apple. Grate a couple of carrots (I find this to be laborious, but don't try to get out of it by chopping the carrots up into little cubes; they have to come out in shaved strips). Chop a cup of fresh celery, about two good-size stalks (throw away the leaves). Add this all together with a half cup of chopped walnuts (or pecans, whatever's handy) and two or three tablespoons of Miracle Whip, enough to lubricate without drowning it. Serve cold. For a different taste, stir in a tablespoon of Realime juice.

▸ GOURMET SALAD

This is also called Dago salad, and I've saved the best for last. This is more of a main course than a side dish, and it's one of God's gifts to men. It goes particularly well with beer and a baseball or football game. Credit for this goes to my friend Joe Buda, a saloon owner in Omaha who also happens to serve the best prime rib in the world.

Now, with Joe Buda's Dago salad, you've got to get into the proper frame of mind. This isn't any good to eat alone; you need a bunch of people who appreciate really fine eating. You also need lots of real tomatoes, so this is more or less a July-through-October dish. Don't try it with store-bought tomatoes; if you can't get homegrown, forget it—you'll just disappoint yourself. Also, you should first locate a couple of loaves of real Italian bread that's *not* sliced. We're talking real crusty stuff here, that you can tear off in hunks and sop in the sauce; none of your old pantywaist white bread. French bread won't quite cut it here, and a hoagie roll is only barely acceptable as an alternative; if you can't find good Italian bread, don't bother with gourmet salad—go fix yourself a peanut butter and jelly.

Gourmet salad is the centerpiece for a meal that includes the unsliced Italian bread, Genoa salami, Capiculla ham, mortadella ham, and provolone cheese. The hams may be a little tricky to locate if you don't have access to an Italian deli. Peppered beef can serve as an acceptable alternative, as can pastrami, but don't be caught serving some bologna or bland cold cuts with this stuff. It's supposed to make you sweat.

Just a note here on human achievement. What are you proud of? Have you benefited mankind in any unique way? Will pilgrims come to your shrine as to Thomas à Becket's?

Me neither. Most of us will have to content ourselves with doing an occasional thing well in a life of not-very-great achievements. Judy and I saved a little neighbor girl's life once; she'd stopped breathing and needed CPR. That *was* a high. I can't think of too many other big deals. Most are fairly little deals. One satisfying moment was hitting the low notes in Vaughan Williams's *Dona Nobis Pacem:* I've been singing with the Omaha Symphonic Chorus. They're tolerant of me and keep me for the few notes I'm good at. At the end of this particular composition there are two optional notes for the second basses: C two octaves below middle C, repeated. I never quite got them in practice, but I nailed them in performance, which I'll probably never be able to do again. The guy next to me whispered, "You *nailed* them!" It was a genuine rush for about four minutes. Now, if I can only bowl a 600 series. Such is the excitement settled for by a person who will never run a four-minute mile, or even an eight-minute mile, for that matter.

Most of our accomplishments are fairly pedestrian, not really worth writing home about. This is *not* the case, however, with Dago salad. Do this well and expect to see it written in the Book of Life when you've gone to your reward. We're talking *excellence* in human affairs here.

Prepare the salad this way: Slice about eight big red, ripe tomatoes into a Dutch oven or other large container. Be sure to cut the tomatoes fairly thin, but don't cut them into horizontal slices; instead, quarter them and then try to get three slices out of each quarter (you'll need patience and a nice sharp knife). Take two large Bermuda (red) onions and slice them *vertically,* not horizontally, so that you get onion pieces that break off into one- or one-and-a-half-inch pieces as the sections separate. Add them to the tomatoes and mix with both hands. Now, add about a cup of garlic-flavored wine vinegar (the garlic-flavored part isn't crucial, but the wine vinegar part is; don't screw up and add white vinegar), a half cup of vegetable oil, a cup of water, a heaping tablespoon of flaked oregano (*not* ground oregano), a tablespoon of *crushed red pepper* (it's available in the spice rack at the store), and a tablespoon of salt. Stir it around thoroughly; it should be the consistency of thick soup or thin stew; if it isn't, add more water—the fluid should just cover the tomatoes and onions. Chill it for about an hour if you can wait that long, then stir it up again and serve it. With this kind of dish, it's best to get right in with both hands and sort of tumble it when you stir; this is particularly gratifying for those of us who like to smear. If you're the kind of person who doesn't like to get his hands into gooey stuff, you probably wouldn't like gourmet salad, anyway. Go eat some dry bread sticks and read your accounting books.

Serve gourmet salad in individual bowls—cereal bowls work better than soup plates; they're generally deeper and can hold more. Most grocery stores sell some very acceptable Styrofoam bowls that hold about ten or twelve ounces, and they can be useful to you if you don't have enough bowls around the house. Let people help themselves—this recipe should be enough for ten people anyway. Take a bowlful of the tomatoes and onions and plenty of juice. Tear off a big handful of the Italian bread, and pick up three or four slices of the hams and the cheese. Eat the salad with a fork, dipping the bread into the juice as you go along and eating the meat and cheese on the side. Serve with lots of cold beer. Glorious, glorious. People will forget the score of the game and won't even care. Have seconds.

▸ BEANS

Baked beans certainly aren't a salad, and they're not a soup either, but they really aren't a main dish, so I'm putting my recipe for beans here as a sort of transitional item because they're good with so many things that constitute a good lunch. Beans with hot dogs, beans with ham, beans on a picnic. They go along with potato salad, coleslaw, that kind of stuff.

"Why do farts smell?"

"So that they can also be enjoyed by the deaf."

You've heard about beans as the musical fruit all your life. I went to my friend Meizenhelder's house one year to watch the Super Bowl, and they served hot dogs with baked beans, a great big plate of deviled eggs, and lots of beer. I went to bed early that night for some reason, and when Judy came into the bedroom, she said, "This place smells like the *zoo.*" The covers were hovering about six inches over me.

I'd heard that adding a little baking soda to baked beans would cut the gas production, so I tried it. Don't bother. You'll have beans that taste like baking soda. Just tough it out: Step up to the farting post and do your duty.

I used to buy a bag of dried navy or great northern beans and soak them overnight, thinking that I was accomplishing something. Forget it; a big can of beans is so cheap that there's no reason to start from scratch. Here's how to go about it: Buy whatever quantity of canned pork and beans you want—let's assume that you want a mess of beans; cut down on the ingredients proportionately if you're just doing a can of beans for three or four people. To feed a bunch, I start with three of the regular cans of Van Camp's pork and beans or whatever's on sale. Open the cans and pour off as much of the juice as you can, dump the beans into a pot, and throw away the little piece of gray fat that they include so that they can use the word *pork* on the label. Fry up about six pieces of bacon until fairly crisp; crumble four of the pieces of bacon into the bean pot, and pour in the bacon grease; save the other two pieces of bacon until later. Chop up a medium onion and throw it in. I used to add a half cup of chopped green pepper as well; I've gotten away from that lately. Add two tablespoons of brown sugar and two tablespoons of white vinegar, about four tablespoons of catsup, and two tablespoons of mustard. Stir it all up and lay the two remaining pieces of bacon across the top. Put the bean pot (you can also use a regular Corning Ware or glass baking dish if you don't have a bean pot) into the oven and bake at low heat (300 degrees) for a couple of hours, poking your head in now and then to enjoy the aroma. Bake until there's a light crust across the top. Serve either hot or cold, however you want. Leftover beans will keep for a long time in the refrigerator.

You can jazz up this basic bean recipe and make it into a main dish, which is handy for feeding a lot of people. Brown a pound or more of ground beef and toss it in with the beans. Cut up eight or ten hot dogs and add them to the baked beans. For a real taste treat, grill some Polish sausage, then cut it up and add it to the basic bean recipe. It will make a hit.

It seems to me that those who cook beans and, as I mention in the next section, soups, have cooking *credibility.* My friend JoAnne tests how good New Orleans cooking is by tasting the beans and rice. I just use beans by themselves as a measure of a cook's sincerity. There's a certain honesty to the plain legume that gives the cook a sort of "I can handle it" impression in the eyes of the observer. Give me somebody who can flat out cook good beans.

We know of any number of would-be cooks who flit back and forth with their one special dish or salad dressing or whatever. It's always some kind of obscure crap that you wouldn't feed to the dog. The guy who makes it inevitably goes on at length about how he had to go to the *strangest* little store to get *just* the right ingredient, and Americans *really* don't know what they're missing, and the cracked capers available in most stores *simply* are unacceptable, and on and on.

This is not a cook.

Should you have the misfortune to have to go to this guy's place for dinner, bring along a package of peanut butter crackers. For one thing, you won't get to eat until after ten.

Contrast this with the guy who really *is* a cook. How can you tell the difference? The real cook can, and does, make beans. Also, from doing roughly six hundred meals during the past year, he's got some sense of what he can do and where his limitations are. He has credibility.

Credibility in general does not come easily. One of the people we had on our faculty was a short person. Looking down on the top of her head one day, I spied a gray hair. She said to leave it, it gave her credibility. That led to a discussion of how short people don't get much respect. We prejudge and make decisions on the most superficial of criteria. Another example: One of my students has lovely platinum-blonde hair, the kind most people would kill for. She says it drives her crazy. No one takes her seriously. I guess they figure that a blonde can't have good sense (she in fact is one bright student). I allowed as how I was willing to trade in my gray hair with a bald spot in the middle and give up a little credibility along with it. Strange. We've got a student who's in a wheelchair. Says he doesn't mind being disabled so much as he hates it when people assume that he's deaf, too; people lean over and yell when they're talking to him, as if having gimpy legs has influenced his ability to hear. I was in our local Perkins Pancake House recently, and four blind people were making their way out; I asked if they needed any help. They said thanks, no, they'd counted their steps. At which point I said, "Well, if I see you guys step in front of an oncoming train, I'll scream on your behalf." They laughed, appreciating being treated like other humans, but the other diners looked at me like I'd just arrived from the moon ("He actually *spoke* to those blind people").

Where was I? Ah, yes: credibility. One sure way of gauging the honesty of a cook is to assess his beans. If they're any good, you can be pretty sure that this isn't just some upstart who makes a mushroom omelet once every eight weeks and claims to be a real cook.

▸ SOUPS

Making soup is much easier than you might think if you've never done it before. When you make homemade soup, you start to get the feeling that you are really *cooking.* Now, we're not going to get into fancypants stuff like vichyssoise or bisques; when I think of soup, I've got in mind something with some oomph to it, stick-to-your-ribs food that you can make a real meal out of. Let's start with basics.

▸ VEGETABLE-BEEF

I happen to admire Campbell's vegetable-beef soup. In fact, I think Campbell's does a hell of a job with soup. However, there are some times when you've got leftover roast beef on your hands and you don't know what else to do with it. Also, homemade soup *is* kind of special, and it gets the kitchen smelling nice. Start with your leftover roast beef or pot roast (just a piece or two won't do; you'll need at least a pound of meat after it's trimmed; about two cupfuls would be better) trim the fat off and save a couple of the nice big pieces of fat. Cut up the lean beef into tiny cubes—less than one-half inch on a side. Put them into a Dutch oven or big soup pot and add two quarts of water. Start it on low heat while you go about preparing the other ingredients. Add the pieces of fat you've saved to the water (you'll be fishing them out later, so use only one or two big pieces). If you've got such a lean roast to start with that there *is* no fat, put about a quarter of a stick of butter into the water with the beef. Add a tablespoon of salt and a teaspoon of black pepper. Chop up two celery stalks into relatively small pieces and dump them in. Do the same with a large yellow onion. If you've got garden tomatoes coming out your ears, peel and chop up about six good ones. (*How to peel a tomato:* With a tea strainer or pair of tongs, dip each tomato into boiling water for about ten seconds; let it sit on the counter until it's cool enough to work with; the skin will come off in your fingers—there's no need to peel them with a knife. Cut the stem part out, and you're ready to go.) If you don't have fresh tomatoes (you don't really need fresh ones for this), get one of the big cans of tomatoes, cut each tomato into quarters, and dump them in along with their juice. Peel and dice two or three carrots and two or three potatoes; in they go. Add a small can of peas (drained) if you like, or a can of green beans, or both. If you want to go wild, they sell little packages of alphabet noodles at most groceries; get some and amuse the kids. Add a quarter teaspoon of garlic powder, a half teaspoon of dried sage, and a quarter teaspoon of dried thyme. Stir it all up thoroughly and float a couple of bay leaves on the top. Cover and let it simmer over low heat for a couple of hours, stirring every so often. After it's cooked for a while, give it a taste. You may want to add more salt or more of the other spices to give it more zip. If you've screwed up and it's way too salty for you already, chop up another potato or two, throw this in, and let it cook for at least another half hour. The extra potato will take the excess salt taste out of the soup. Stir it up and see if its consistency suits you. I like thick soup, but you may want to add more water. You can keep this stuff going on low heat all day long if you wish, particularly if you want to impress your friends. ("What's that great smell?" "Oh, just a little homemade soup I whipped up.") Before serving, fish out what's left of the pieces of fat and also toss out the bay leaves. Stir it up one more time and serve it good and hot.

▸ BEAN SOUP

This is a really easy way to do a relatively exotic soup that folks will be wild over. Start with two cans of Campbell's bean with bacon soup; toss them in a pot and add just one canful of water. Heat it up, and in the meantime dice a medium-size onion into tiny pieces. Add a tablespoon of Worcestershire sauce and a cup of red wine (the cheaper the better) to the hot soup just before serving. Ladle out into bowls and sprinkle the chopped onion over the top.

▸ CHICKEN SOUP

Don't mess with chicken soup. Nobody has enough leftover chicken to make soup with, and there's no sense in buying a whole chicken just to make soup. Enjoy your mother's chicken soup.

▸ TURKEY SOUP

You occasionally have all kinds of leftover turkey. Trim the carcass, though, when you're making soup; you'll only need the little hunks for this—save those bigger leftover slices for tetrazzini. Try to come up with about two cups of shreds and leavings. Put them in a bowl in the refrigerator. Then, put the carcass itself into a big pot or Dutch oven, cover it with water, put on the lid, and simmer.If you happen to have saved any of the juicier pieces of the skin, particularly from off the back down to the pope's nose, toss that in as well. Cook over medium-low heat (not enough to bring on a heavy boil) for several hours. Then uncover, fish out the bones and what's left of the skin, and shake back into the water any loose meat scraps that are still clinging to the bones. You have just made turkey stock. Bend down and see if there are any nice, shiny globules of fat floating on the top. If there really aren't many, add a couple of pats of butter or margarine. Throw away the bones and skin.

Now toss your trimmed turkey meat that you've been saving into the hot stock. Add a tablespoon of salt, a teaspoon of pepper, and a quarter teaspoon of dried sweet basil. Add a teaspoon of chopped, dried parsley if you've got it, but don't make a special trip to the store if you don't. Cut up three or four carrots into small cubes and a good-size yellow onion; toss them in. Float a bay leaf on top; simmer. About fifteen minutes before you want to serve it, cook a small package of egg noodles in a separate pot, following the directions on the label. Drain and rinse the noodles with hot water after they're tender, then add them to the soup. Stir it up and add more salt and pepper to taste. Add more water if it's gotten too thick. As an alternative to the noodles, you can use rice. Follow the directions on a package of Minute Rice to come out with about two cupsful. Add the cooked rice just before you're ready to serve the soup. Pull out the bay leaf and throw it away. Serve the soup thick and hot.

▸ SPLIT PEA SOUP

This same recipe is also good for lentil soup, so if you're color-blind and have grabbed the wrong package at the store, don't worry—proceed with vigor. Both split pea soup and lentil soup are thick and hearty, and they go good with French bread for the central part of a meal in winter that will give you courage to shovel some more snow.

Both split peas and lentils come dried in little plastic packages; they look pretty much the same, except that the peas are obviously green and the lentils are brown. They of course taste different, but both soups are essentially similar. Here goes:

Soak a package of the dried peas or lentils in two quarts of water overnight in a Dutch oven or other large pot. They ought to soften up some and swell slightly. The next day, pour off the water through a colander and rinse the peas and rinse your Dutch oven. Then dump the rinsed peas back into the pot, add two quarts of fresh water, and put it on low heat, covered. We'll go on the assumption that you have some leftover ham, and that's the reason that you thought of soup in the first place. You'll need about two cups of trimmed ham, cut into small cubes (trimmed leftover roast beef will do just fine if you're making lentil soup; you're supposed to use beef for lentil soup, but ham is just fine; on the other hand, I'm not too sure about beef in split pea soup). Trim the meat, chop it up into a bowl, and put it into the refrigerator until later.

Now dice up a medium-large onion, three stalks of celery, and three or four carrots; toss them in with the peas. Add a teaspoon of pepper, two teaspoons of salt, a half teaspoon of garlic powder, and a quarter teaspoon of dried thyme. Stir it all together, float two bay leaves on the top, cover, and simmer over low heat for two hours. If you've got a ham bone (does anyone bake whole hams anymore?), toss it in as well. Simmering all this stuff together should start to mush it up; if things are still fairly crunchy after two hours, stir it again, turn up the heat slightly, and simmer for another two hours. Now here comes the tricky part, and lucky for you it's optional: Turn off the heat, toss out the bay leaves and the ham bone, and pour the whole mess through a sieve into another large pot or saucepan. The water will pour through and the peas and other vegetables will stay behind in the sieve. *Force them through* it (the back of a large wooden spoon works well for this), so it's coming out of the bottom of the sieve in a thick paste that's plopping back into the water. This is really a disgusting sight, but it smells much better than changing a messy diaper and you got through *that* all right.

If you don't have a sieve, a really big tea strainer will do, but a colander won't work for this task. If you absolutely refuse to get involved in a mess like this, you don't have to do it. While to be strictly legal, both lentil and split pea soups should be done this way, you've got two other options:

1. Tough it out and have chunky split pea soup. That is, don't worry about the texture—you've cooked the hell out of this stuff, and it ought to be soft enough to eat without the mushing-up process. So what if the soup doesn't have the consistency of library paste?

2. Find an alternative to putting the soup through a sieve. One way is to pour almost all of the water through a colander into another pot, holding back about a quarter of it. Then send the peas, vegetables, and remaining water through a blender (you may have to take it in two loads), and then pour the ground-up paste in with the remaining water.

I personally would rather mess with the sieve than clean the goo out of my blender. But, God made these machines to help us, and you might want to try this route. It works.

Now, whether you've made mush out of the peas or not, you're past a decision point and ready to proceed. Add the chopped-up ham or beef. Taste it and add additional spices if you find the soup too bland (go easy on the salt; you're up shit creek if you get this stuff too salty, and the ham will add some saltiness to the soup). Make a decision on consistency; if it's thinner than you like it, simmer for another hour with the lid off; if it's too thick for your taste, gradually stir in more water and simmer for another half hour with a lid on it. I like my soup nice and thick, but this is a matter both of individual taste and of how many people you've got to feed.

What to *do* with lentil or split pea soup after you've cooked it presents a problem. I love the stuff, but three nights in a row is all I can handle. Judy will take some to be polite and then kind of poke at it, apparently thinking she's fooling me into the belief that she's actually eating it (I'll admit it: By agreeing to have me do the cooking, the woman *has* had to pay a price). And, I'll have to be honest, split pea soup *is* just plain ugly.

Back when I thought I could afford *Geo* magazine, I was thoroughly taken with one of their articles on cosmetic surgery. It featured this guy in California who rakes in bucks by landscaping faces that God has screwed up. As plastic surgeons go, this fellow was *good.* The article featured a series of before-and-after pictures. One woman in particular, I must confess, was a sad case in the "before" pictures. You could look up *ugly* in the dictionary and there'd be her picture. Well, this doc carved some off her nose and put some back on her chin, took a nip and a tuck here and there, and in the "after" pictures had her looking better than a thoroughbred racehorse. To my utter shame and horror, I found myself *liking* her better. Here was this woman I didn't know from a load of hay, and I *liked* her better when she wasn't ugly. A commentary on our values.

It's kind of that way with lentil soup.

If your kids are like mine, they won't eat much split pea or lentil soup; they'll say it looks yukky. What can you expect from a generation that was raised on Fruit Loops? The principal nutrient that my two boys received for their first decade of life was red dye number two. Split pea soup may lack glamour, but it makes up for it with substance. It's an acquired taste, and you'll have to beat down their natural resistance through constant repetition. That means that you're going to have to store some or most of this stuff, unless you're feeding it to fourteen guys who are full of beer, a group of people who, it has been proven, will eat just about anything. Storing it, in this case, means freezing it.

▸ SOME THOUGHTS ON TUPPERWARE

I don't like, as a matter of policy, things that your wife bought from some other guy's wife at a house party. This goes for Amway products, Mary Kay cosmetics, or Tupperware. I'm not saying that the products are bad, or that they're a bad value. I just don't like the element of social pressure entering into the purchasing transaction; I think that gives the merchant something of an advantage over the consumer. I've seen it any number of times: My wife comes home with some useless doodad that she'd never have dreamed of buying in the store, and she'll look at me in explanation, "Sally was having a party, and I felt like I had to buy *something.*" To me, that's a less-than-honest buyer-seller transaction. The people I've seen who are really sold on these home-sale kinds of products are usually the people who are selling them, or who have a bunch of their own stringers somewhere down the pyramid who are selling for them. They get to be what Eric Hoffer called True Believers, and they wind up boring the pants off you, telling you how great Amway shoe polish is and how it will make your shoes last longer, look great, and make you a finer person overall. Who *gives* a shit?

Now, this isn't an original line with me, but it's one that's good enough to repeat. Freud asked the great question: "What does woman *want?*" The great answer: "Tupperware!"

My general policy of despising home-sale products is somewhat moderated in the case of Tupperware storage containers (their plastic grapefruit knife isn't bad, either). If it weren't for the manner of the purchase, in fact, I'd be pretty much sold on the stuff. They make a quart and a quart-and-a-half square plastic container with covers that actually fit without cracking and that give a tight seal, perfect for freezing soup. If your family is like mine and only half of the soup sells, you'll have to freeze some of it. I use the Tupperware containers, and my freezer is gradually filling up with half loads of soup that I like a lot and that the rest of the family only tolerates to humor me. A pointer: Put a piece of masking tape on the top of your container and write on it the date that you made the soup. In case you really have any intention at all of getting the stuff out of the freezer and warming it up, you'll at least have a fighting chance of keeping your stock in some kind of reasonable rotation. Frozen soup tends to lose its zip after the third year.

When my friend Chuck died (he was the guy with the eggbeater), we helped his wife clean out his stuff. Chuck was a saver. A good bit of what we cleaned out was food that he'd put into the freezer sometime back in the Kennedy administration. I don't know whether or not it tasted good.

Judy saves stuff, too. Not food, but *stuff.* She likes stuff. Every now and again she'll go through a closet and weed out several lawn-and-leaf bags full of stuff, and the Salvation Army thrift store will be able to restock for another couple of months. I made the mistake, early on in our marriage, of helping dispose of some of Judy's stuff. I suppose I should have waited for her to get home and maybe get some kind of approval for the things I pitched. Not doing so didn't promote matrimonial harmony.

One reason, I think, that she's never tossed *me* out is that neither of us hits as hard as we can. I learned this growing up with an older brother in the house. By the time I was fourteen, I was a good deal bigger than him, but I never hit him (or anyone else that I can recall) as hard as I could. I didn't really want to *hurt* anyone. Conscious of the fact that I can have a vile temper, I at least try to keep it from building up to such a point that I actually have to *destroy* the other person. Judy's the same way: Fight, yes; kill, no.

I think a lot of couples don't know how to fight. They keep a lid on it, pretending that everything's going all right; then, when it finally blows, the only fit retribution is death itself. Go for the jugular. I'm not necessarily talking about physical violence, more about other things that may be equally destructive. Sticks and stones may break my bones, but names will *kill* me. Instead of having a series of skirmishes, and opportunities to make up, they wait until they have to drop the atom bomb. There's no sense in getting all worked up over a bunch of *stuff.* One must learn to pull one's punches. If the stuff you're saving is food, use Tupperware.

Did all of the Tupperware leave as a part of the settlement? Search about the supermarket for Rubbermaid products; they're just fine.

CHAPTER 3

Little Stuff

▸ LITTLE STUFF

If you're like me, finger sandwiches made out of cream cheese are not high on your list of basic nutrients. Read the food pages in your local newspaper once in a while, and you'll find six exciting ways to make cucumber dip and pumpkin roll-ups.

Sorry, none of that for me. I'll take beer and pizza, thank you.

Some people can take an extraordinary amount of time when they entertain. I'm more likely than not to put the booze and an ice bucket out on the kitchen counter, put a few bowls of pretzels around the living room, and relax and enjoy the company. A famous hostess was once asked what her secret was, since she threw such great parties. Her reply: "Whiskey and peanuts." I think the old girl hit the nail on the head.

Now, it may happen that you want to fix some light snacks or munchies for guests, and I'm going to give you a few tried-and-tested winners. I put these things under the heading of "Little Stuff" because they don't exactly fit with lunch and they come before dinner.

Let's assume that you already know how to put out a few bowls of nuts or some ripple chips with onion dip. Don't get caught making your own chip dip—they sell a dozen different kinds at the dairy counter in the store, and virtually every one of them is better than what you might whip up with some sour cream and onion soup mix, and they cost less, too. A variation on the chip-dip routine that's really nothing new but provides a nice change is a raw-vegetable plate with a couple of different kinds of dip. Just cut up some celery and carrot sticks, slice a cucumber, maybe some small pieces of raw broccoli or cauliflower, and add a touch of green onions, pickles, and olives on the side. The raw cauliflower in onion dip, or raw broccoli in horseradish dip in particular, are both better than you might suspect and are easy and quick to prepare. They'll also make a hit with your organic friends who are into bean sprouts and tofu.

Little stuff on a cracker usually sells well. Don't bother doing the work yourself; just set out a basketful of crackers (use your imagination and get something more exotic than Saltines), a knife and a small summer sausage or hard salami, plus maybe a pound of Edam or Gouda cheese, or all of the above. Whip up some tuna spread and put it out in a small bowl with a fork and let folks smear it on a cracker. It's good therapy for them, gives them something to do. Spread some pimiento cheese or some peanut butter down the middle of some celery sticks. Throw all of this together and you'll have a nice spread. We have wowed our friends at a Christmas party for the past few years by putting out all this easy stuff plus some cookies surrounding a whole smoked turkey. We just set out the cooked smoked turkey with a butcher knife and let them go after it. By the end of the evening it's been nibbled down to the bones, and everybody thinks it's so great and that we went to so much trouble.

I'm here to tell you that a smoked turkey is no trouble at all. *Hamburgers* are more trouble than smoked turkey. Just look in the freezer section at the market where they have the regular frozen turkeys. Look! Some of them are smoked! If your store doesn't sell them, ask the butcher. They're easily available, and he can get you one in a few days. Swift markets them nationally, and so do a number of other meat packers. Just follow the directions on the label: Stick it in a pan, put it in the oven, bake it for a few hours, and that's it. Serve it when it's cooled down. You don't have to do anything, really, but stick the thing in the oven; you don't have to stuff it, you don't have to baste it; just cook it. You don't even have to slice the thing; your guests will do that and have a good time digging away at it. You're a great host.

There are a few other things that make for good finger food; they take a little more work, but not much:

▸ DEVILED EGGS

Deviled eggs are great with a spread for a party, on a picnic, or with lunch. The hard part is boiling and getting the shells off the eggs without destroying them, but you already know how to do that by following our hot-cold-hot-water routine. Boil up a dozen eggs and peel them. Slice them in half the long way and gently flop the yolks out into a bowl, leaving the cooked whites with a nice round crater in them. Now slice up a half of a yellow onion *very* finely; chop up the thin slices into tiny little pieces; add the chopped onion to the egg yolks. Also add two tablespoons of Miracle Whip, a tablespoon of mustard, a teaspoon of Worcestershire sauce, and a teaspoon of salt. Mix all of this up until the yolks are smooth, about the consistency of wet plaster. If it's too thick and there's not enough moisture, leaving the yolks still a little crumbly, add a little more Miracle Whip. Mixing this stuff up with a fork seems to work better than with a spoon. Now, when the yellow goo is nice and smooth, spoon it back into the egg halves. You'll have plenty to give it a generous treatment, a nice mound of the stuff. I've seen this done with a pastry bag, but I wouldn't bother with that unless I was making deviled eggs for the graduating class at West Point. Now, when you've gotten all of the yolk mix spooned into the whites, shake just a little paprika over each of them. Refrigerate and serve them cold.

▸ CHEESE BREADS

I'm at a loss as to what to call these. In our house we call them Barbie Johnson's cheese-and-olive-and-onion-and-curry things on rye bread, which is, I'll admit, quite a cumbersome title. Barbie Johnson, a dear friend, taught me how to make them. She and her husband, Gene, a beloved professor emeritus at the University of Georgia, used to have some great garden parties. Not everything to eat was as good as this, mind you. I remember some sort of popovers that were brought by the wife of one of the Pakistani graduate students. They looked okay, so I bit into one of them and then started looking for the fire extinguisher. Santa Maria! Those things were hot enough to melt rocks. This guy laughed and said, "In my country, it's not a good meal unless your shirt is wet by the end of it." I can't say that I saw the humor at the time. I pitched the rest of the thing over the garden wall, and about thirty seconds later heard this,

"Yip! Yip!" We looked over the wall and saw a dog running in circles.

Well, that wasn't Barbie's fault, and here's her recipe for some really good hot hors d'oeuvres: Get yourself two loaves of that little cocktail bread that Pepperidge Farm puts out. I like to use one loaf of the dark rye and another loaf of the pumpernickle. Spread the individual pieces of bread out on cookie sheets. Now grate a pound of Colby cheese (mild Cheddar will work just as well, but I like Colby better) into a bowl, being careful not to run your finger along the food grater and mess up the cheese. Dice a medium-size yellow onion into fairly small pieces and add it to the grated cheese. Add two of the small (4¼ ounces) cans of chopped ripe olives, a teaspoon of curry powder, and two tablespoons of Miracle Whip. Stir it all up and put about a teaspoon of this mélange on each piece of bread. Put the cookie sheets into a fairly hot oven (400 degrees or so) for five or six minutes until the cheese melts. Serve them hot to a grateful public.

This recipe, by the way, is for a multitude. If you've only got eight or ten people to serve them to, cut the recipe in half.

▸ PIZZA BREADS

This can work equally well as finger food for a party or as a main dish. I've quit making regular pizza because this is so much better and so much easier. Start with a loaf of sliced Italian bread. If you can't find substantial, crusty Italian bread where you are, split English muffins would work for this. Get a jar of Ragu' Pizza Quick at the store; it's in the same place that they have prepared spaghetti sauce. There are different flavors of Pizza Quick: plain, with meat, with mushrooms, and with pepperoni; suit yourself. I think the pepperoni flavor has more zip. You'll also need one of the sixteen-ounce packages of grated mozzarella cheese, and one of those packages of grated Parmesan cheese plus a pound of bulk sausage and a small can of mushroom stems and pieces.

Crumble up the sausage into a frying pan and start to brown it over medium heat. If you want to be authentic, you can buy a package of six Italian sausages instead of the pound of bulk sausage. If you do, slice the skins off of them with a sharp knife and crumble them up into the frying pan. Either kind of sausage works fine. While the sausage is cooking, open the can of mushrooms and pour off the fluid in the can, then toss them in with the sausage. Cook until nice and brown and then suck the grease out with a turkey baster.

In the meantime, pour the Pizza Quick out into a flat bowl and just drop each bread slice or muffin individually into it, coating one side of the bread evenly with the sauce. Arrange the breads on cookie sheets. Spoon the sausage-mushroom mix onto them after it's cooked, then sprinkle the grated mozzarella over the top of each. You'll have plenty of mozzarella to go around, but you'll have to experiment at first to see how much to put on each slice; it comes out to about two teaspoons of cheese per slice, but you can't do this job with a spoon—it's finger work. Then sprinkle a generous amount of the Parmesan cheese on top of the mozzarella. Pop the cookie sheets into a medium oven, about 350 degrees, for five or six minutes: long enough to melt the cheese and put a light brown crust on the bottoms of the bread slices. If you go too long and the bread bottoms are black, feed it to the dog and try again.

If you're serving this as finger food, cut each slice into quarters with a sharp knife; otherwise, serve them whole. *Mamma mia!*

Commercially available snack food often takes a bad

rap. People put their collective noses in the air and sniff at "junk food." I'm not so sure I go along with that: To me, junk food is something that's just been sprayed with chlordane, or food that's starting to rot. (One overlooked function of food preservatives: They keep you from dying.) I plan to set out a tray of Twinkies the next time I entertain, just to see how they'll sell. We have friends who became parents later in life and are thus demented. Mistaking my vacant look for an indication of interest, the woman told me at length how she'd shopped around for day care where they gave the kids raisins for snacks instead of junk food. Not wishing to prolong the conversation any more than was absolutely necessary, I neglected to mention to her the report I'd just read indicating that raisins are at the very top of the list of things that rot kids' teeth (they're full of sugar, and they stick). She'd probably take the poor kid to a place where they snack on celery, which has no calories at all. Talk about junk food.

Yankees don't know about gourmet junk food. Back in 1967, when we were young, Judy and I lived in Mooresville, North Carolina. Nice little town. Friendly people. Nothing to do. The Whataburger was the only thing open after 6:00 P.M., and I was introduced there to a southern art form, the Moon Pie. The Moon Pie is like the Georgia Belle peach or the Vidallia onion: too good to share. They eat them all in the South and don't tell anyone else. A Moon Pie is a sort of big, round cookie covered with marshmallow and chocolate. A delight to both the eye and the palate. I've liked North Carolina ever since. Serve some at your next party.

I think that about 90 percent of the reason for the brisk sales of Perrier water and Brie is that we are so astonishingly obsessed with impressing each other. This is, of course, just another variation on the "Mommie, look at *me!*" bumper sticker: "Colorado Native" (now *there's* an accomplishment in human affairs), "Baby on Board" (great, you've mastered a considerable level of skill). Ernest Becker would say that this is all a manifestation of death anxiety. ("Look at me! I *exist*! I have French mineral water!")

The fact that we do exist is, of course, not really too important in the larger scheme of things, which is pretty frustrating when you realize it. Maybe this lack of meaning underlies the national obsession to exist a little *longer*. I think it would be great to have "This guy was *really* healthy" written on your tombstone. I ride my Schwinn Air Dyne like a madman every night. I'm not quite sure for what. For one thing, I'm not aware of any *real* research proving that exercise makes you live much longer. Okay, so my odds of having a coronary are lower; does that mean I won't die of something else? Can you add one cubit to your height or one year to your life? If you can, what meaningful thing will you do with an extra year of old age? He who dies with the most toys wins.

The presentation of self in everyday life, which is a principal preoccupation for most of us (I have a sister-in-law who actually hid her face once when I was taking pictures; she didn't have her makeup on) is a *strain* after a while. Impression management, a major American industry, eventually gets us *nervous.* Politicians must have a terrible time of it, wondering what everyone is thinking of them all the time. Nobody seems to value being laid-back anymore. Maybe the next candidate should give this a try: "Fairly honest government on the days when I'm working at it." Alistair Cooke explains the reason that Warren Harding, an idiot, was such a popular president after Woodrow Wilson, Ph.D.: "After an eight-year audience with an archbishop, the country wanted to have a beer with a pal."

So, throw caution to the winds, toss out your French mineral water, and serve your friends Blatz beer and malted milk balls. Who cares what the neighbors think?

CHAPTER 4

Dinner

A lot of the stuff we've talked about already goes just as well for dinner as it does for lunch. Salads, for example, and soups are just as appropriate at dinnertime as they are any other time of the day. The same goes for the Little Stuff, and some of the side dishes, such as beans or potato salad, as well. Generally, though, when I think of dinner, I see a main meat dish with a bunch of other stuff, which leads us to:

▸ BREAD AND ROLLS

I usually look at bread as the first thing to give up whenever I'm trying to lose weight; bread is pretty heavy in calories, given that it doesn't provide all *that* much pleasure. I don't diet too often, actually; I just throw in the towel and enjoy myself most times. There really is, if you stop to think about it, an unusual egocentricity to the frame of thinking that somebody else actually cares much what you look like. Will you be a better *person* if there's twenty pounds less of you?

A couple of my younger students at the university were smiling the other day as I struggled to take the rubbers off my shoes, it being a snowy day. I said to them, "There comes a point in life when being young and cool isn't nearly so important as having warm, dry feet." I'd make a lousy yuppie.

I doubt that they much got the point; I increasingly find myself playing to the older students. The composition of many universities has changed over the past couple of decades, and there now are a lot of "nontraditional" students in the classroom. That's especially true on our Omaha campus, where the average age is a full eight years older than on our campus in Lincoln. As a result, we have a lot of people here who have some miles on them; they tend to be pretty interesting as individuals.

Not that the Tammies and Debbies aren't interesting. It's swell to listen to one of these kids talk about working on her tan.

I shouldn't make fun. But what the hell. A few years ago *The Lou Grant Show* featured a segment concerning a twenty-two-year-old who was trying to seduce the character played by Ed Asner, figuring to get herself a job on the paper. When he finally realized what was going on, he said, "My dear, I'm too *old* for you. For us to have a decent argument, I'd have to explain both sides of it to you." My friend Diane and I were talking to each other at a party. Looking over at some younger folk, she said, "I'd sure like to take him out and fuck him." Pause for effect. "I wouldn't care to *talk* to him, you understand."

Well, we have plenty of people who are interesting to talk to, who enjoy a good dinner roll, and who see the value of having warm, dry feet. Several, in fact, have given me thoughts and suggestions for this effort along the way, and I appreciate their help.

In the year 2040, the three most common names for senior citizens will be Tammie, Debbie, and Muffin.

But I seem to have digressed. The virtue of a good dinner roll is that it adds substance to the meal. When I was an undergraduate, the favored place for many of us to eat was the grill at the local bowling alley. The food wasn't really all that terrific, but two thick slices of homemade bread came along with it. Everyone waddled out with a full, satisfied feeling.

Making homemade bread goes beyond the ambition of this book, although it's not really all *that* difficult. However, our purpose is to make you look good without working you to death, and I have vivid memories of my teenage years, knocking out three hundred loaves of bread every Saturday morning down at the Country Maid Bakery for a munificent $1.25 per hour. That was *work.* My aversion to honest toil is the main reason that I took up professoring. If you are, in fact, bound and determined to make your own bread, good luck to you. You're on your own.

Well, all right. Here's the no-sweat way to do it, seeing that you're just in a real sweat to murder a bunch of yeast. If you *must* have that fresh-bread aroma to impress the latest contestant in the divorcee derby, there's an easy way to go about it. Hie you to the freezer section at the local supermarket. They sell frozen bread dough there, all made up into loaves already. Just thaw and bake, it's as easy as that. Watch the company moon about it when you pop out the bread you've baked yourself. Glory be.

A very wise realtor (is that an oxymoron?) once told me that the smell of fresh bread was one of the real kickers in selling a house. The others: cut the grass, paint the inside walls white, store half of the furniture, and get rid of the dog.

Anyway, that smell of fresh bread is a potent persuader, and you might just need all the help you can get, regardless of what you're selling.

One small tip on the frozen-bread-dough route: Be sure it's thawed through and through. Don't expect much more than a hard little lump if you bake it two hours after getting it out of the freezer; the stuff needs time to get to room temperature and rise. Take it out of the plastic wrapper, put a clean dish towel over it, and let it thaw out overnight. Also, just before you pop it into the hot oven (that's right, get the oven hot *before* you put the bread into it), slit the top of the loaf with a sharp knife and paint the top with melted butter or margarine. This will enhance both the color and the smell.

Enough about baking bread, which I didn't plan to get into, anyway. Most any bread needs can be met at the bakery, or the bakery section of the food store; that's what they're there for. Be assured that you'll impress nobody with white factory bread. I think the days are past when the rule of thumb was that the upper classes ate hard rolls and the lower classes ate soft rolls, but I think that most guests like a piece of bread they can get their teeth into. (I just love the ad on TV that has this dippy woman going on about these little prepackaged cupcakes and stuffed sponge cakes—she's rotting the teeth out of her kids' heads with the crap, but in the commercial she's goo-gooing over how great it is because the stuff is really *fresh:* "I know that my family thrives on Gloperoos because they're really *fresh.*"Then she gives a self-satisfied grin, like she's just won the Mother of the Year prize. She could be feeding the brats fresh dog shit, and it would have about as much virtue. "It's so *fresh!*") Let's assume that most of us have moved out of the psychology of the Great Depression, and eating stale bread is no longer an issue.

Fresh, homemade biscuits will really wow your guests, and they're not nearly so hard to prepare as you'd think. Just get a box of Bisquick and follow the directions. Work the water into the mix with a fork, sprinkle a little flour on the countertop—and on your hands—and get in there. You don't even have to roll the dough out with a rolling pin (although there's no reason to be scared of the thing; give it a try—it's kind of fun). Just flatten out the blob to the thickness of a half to three quarters of an inch. Cut out the biscuits with a small juice glass. Pop the biscuits onto a cookie sheet. Re-form the dough that's left after the first run-through, and do it again. They'll take about eight or ten minutes to bake, and you want to serve these little suckers while they're nice and hot, so plan to do this last as you're preparing the meal. Biscuits stay warmer when they're wrapped up in a small towel in a little basket. Serve with real butter and strawberry preserves. Eat, drink, and be merry.

We'll get back to baking more exotic stuff when we discuss desserts. For now, though, let's get to that other item that'll stick to your ribs as well as your hips:

▸ THE POTATO

Humble they may be, but my friend Goldie built an honest life around the common potato for eighty-nine years. I'm not too hung up on potatoes, and I will admit that they're the second thing I give up, after bread, when dieting. On the other hand, they go so well with almost everything, and they're so cheap and full of vitamins, it's hard to get along without them.

Now, I have nothing against the red potato as a matter of policy, but I will admit that I find myself consistently buying the brown Idaho potatoes because they're more versatile; you can bake them (baking a red potato seems odd to me) in addition to all the other things you can do with any other kind of potato. There is no reason to buy two kinds if one will do.

The baked potato is absolutely the easiest side dish in any dinner, and it goes with 'most everything. Just wash however many of them you plan to serve, wrap them individually in aluminum foil, and pop them into a 400-degree oven for an hour. *Voilà.* Serve them in the foil wrappers and have available a stick of butter or margarine, a tub of sour cream, and maybe some bacon bits. Hormel puts out the real kind, which are ever so much better than the soybean kind. Another good thing you can put on a baked potato is crumbled cheese. People like to fix up their own baked potato, and you can let them. It saves you the work.

Our friend Angie was impressed with Pat because he knew all about the business end of a potato masher. We pointed out to her that there wasn't an Irish boy growing up in Chicago when we were kids who *didn't* know everything there was to know about the potato masher, both theory and practice. Now it so happens that mashed potatoes, the other true essential in the potato repertoire, actually do not have to be mashed by hand. I keep my potato masher around to use when I make strawberry jam, and that's the only use it gets. The electric hand mixer is the instrument of choice when it comes to mashing potatoes.

Simply peel one medium-size potato for each of the people you plan to serve. Using a potato peeler is not all that much of an art, once you get used to it; just remember, peel using strokes that are going *away* from you. Don't use a knife when peeling; it's slower and it takes off too much of the potato. After peeling the potatoes, cut them into quarters and boil for twenty or thirty minutes, until they're soft when poked with the tip of a knife. Pour off the water, keeping the boiled-potato pieces in the pot (hold them in with the lid). If you're planning to make gravy, save the water you've boiled the potatoes in. You probably won't need all of it—you should use enough water to cover the top of the potatoes when boiling them—but you will need at least half of it for gravy. Back to the mashed potatoes; we'll do gravy later.

Add about a quarter of a stick of margarine and a few ounces of milk (more if you're making mashed potatoes for an army) and a half teaspoon of salt to the boiled-potato pieces. Immediately start grinding up the whole mess with a hand mixer. These little electric mixers go for less than twenty bucks, and they're too handy to do without. At first the mixing will be a little rough as you break up the potato pieces, but stay with it. After a minute, things will start to smooth out. Add a little milk if they're just too dry, but be careful; you can make potato soup by adding too much milk. Stop after a minute and run a rubber scraper around the sides to get all of the ingredients into the action, then mix away for another minute or so, being careful to get all the lumps out. If you're not serving them right away, you can keep mashed potatoes in a glass bowl in a warm oven (300°); just remember to put the bowl on a hot pad after you take it out.

As an alternative to keeping them hot in the oven, you can do one of two other things (actually, another alternative, as I think of it, is to serve them cold; on the other hand, those who would tell you that there are many fine uses for leftover mashed potatoes are full of baloney):

1. You *can* keep them warm on the stove. Just keep them in the pot in which they were made and keep them covered, on *very* low heat. If you have a gas stove, this will be especially tricky. The very lowest setting on an electric stove burner should be about right. In either case, you'll have to stir them every minute or so to keep them from sticking to the bottom of the pot and scorching. Let us be very clear on this point: You don't want your mashed potatoes to scorch on the bottom. It not only sets off the smoke alarm, but also makes for a pot that's a bitch to clean. Do you enjoy soaking a pot in hot, soapy water for

a couple of hours and then going at it with elbow grease and an SOS pad? I thought not.

2. Your second alternative for keeping mashed potatoes hot is to get your timing down to such a fine degree that virtually everything else in the meal is ready to serve when the potatoes are done. This takes skill, practice, finely honed moves (think of yourself as the Magic Johnson of the kitchen; you're not a klutz, you're an *artist*), and the proper frame of mind. Yes, you too can have everything come out right, at the same time, and tasting good. This takes both a bit of planning and considerable grace, both of which will come in time as you get used to moving around in your kitchen. Even more so, however, it requires confidence and the self-assurance that *you know that you can succeed.* Let us, then, lay the potato aside for the moment and think about something more basic to victory in the kitchen:

▸ PSYCHING YOURSELF UP

When Roscoe Tanner, who went on to have a fair amount of success as a pro, was a college senior, he lost in the final round of the NCAA tennis tournament to an opponent of inferior skill who had, it was clear to all observers, psyched Roscoe out. I was amazed, as I sat in the stands watching Tanner go down in defeat, each time I saw him make one of his blistering serves, to see the other guy (whose name I no longer remember) howl and dance about, screaming, "I can't even *see* the damn thing!" This rattled Roscoe so much that he began to clip the net with his serves and then to take a little bit off of each one. The other guy ultimately won the championship. The point is, he was bold as brass, full of chutzpah, and he acted like he was going to win. Acting like you're going to win when cooking a dinner is important. However, psyching yourself up goes beyond just pretending.

Should you ever have had the occasion to look up something in the psychology section of the library, you may have noticed that the psychology books are shelved right next to the philosophy books. There's a reason for this. The first psychologists *were* philosophers, and *psyche* translates from the Greek as "soul." (The word for "mind" or "wits" is *phrenes,* thus *schizophrenia*—"split personality.") So, in a sense, psychology is the study of the soul. To "psych" yourself up, then, gets into an area of thought where you're looking for real meaning in life. This isn't as heavy-duty as it sounds, so stick with me for a moment. One way of finding out what's really meaningful in your life, I tell my students, is to think of what you'd like to be remembered for. I'm talking about cutting through the crap now; think of what will appear on your tombstone ("Here lies a guy who owned a BMW"). Victor Frankl tells us that people find meaning in their families, in human relationships, in their accomplishments. Think of those times in your life that are really warm memories, satisfying times with people that you love.

I'll bet that food was involved in some way.

Sitting around the dinner table, sharing family stories, joking with each other, arguing, celebrating a holiday, giving a party—all of these times for really meaningful human relationships focus around food. Passover, Christmas, Thanksgiving, birthday celebrations: What would they be without a meal? Which would you rather have on your tombstone: "Here lies the author of ad copy for Brillo pads" or "Here lies one hell of a cook who made a lot of people happy"?

Serving a good dinner combines an opportunity for really satisfying human relationships with an area of genuine achievement. So, not only should you not be afraid of getting into the kitchen and digging right in, you should also see it as something that over the years will add meaning to your life. Psyching yourself up to throw a good dinner on the table involves getting your head straight, but it also does something good for your *soul.*

So let's think, for a bit, about strategy and getting your act together so that the biscuits, the potatoes, the meat, and the veggies all come out at the same time. If you're the compulsive sort who demands perfection in everything you do, it's my sad duty to tell you that you've purchased the wrong book. Donate it to the library and take the purchase price off your taxes as a contribution (in our case, it's probably pretty doubtful that this is an asset that has appreciated as a work of art, so don't press your luck). Let's go so far as to assume that you're neither compulsive nor the kind of guy who'd really just as soon go hungry. You've got the basic motivation to cook; perhaps for yourself, perhaps for a bunch of people every now and again.

Your goal is to get everything you're cooking coordinated to such a degree that it's all ready to serve at pretty much the same time. Some years back I had the pleasure of eating a banquet meal at a Chinese commune up-country from Shanghai. Now, they *did* serve us one whole hell of a lot of food ("Clean up your plate, Joe, there are people starving in Kansas City"). There was a total of twenty-three different dishes. I suppose that it doesn't matter that two separate servings of green beans and two trips with the watermelon, both of which were in season, counted as four dishes. No need to be picky. They'd serve something—and all of it was good—and we'd eat it and then wait around for what came next. It was increasingly obvious, though, that the cooks didn't have much of a *plan* for the meal. They'd just cook something, see how it went, and then think up something else. Nothing against the Chinese, who were magnificent hosts; it's just that this particular bunch of cooks didn't have their act together in terms of *timing.* Making lots of long-winded toasts serves an important function in these kinds of situations. The cooks get a chance to whip up something else.

The point is, of course, that you'll want to have some sort of a notion of what you're going to serve, how long it will take to cook, and in what order things are to come. Let's start with a simple, well-rounded meal (this means that if you eat this way, your body will be well-rounded after a while). I am, by the way, heartened with the new wave of TV commercials that have been featuring a group of phonies sitting around brainstorming the design for a new car or computer system. They've got the obligatory woman and the representative racial minority (who in this case owns the company) in the group, of course. Actually my personal hope is to someday have a car that has been designed by a planning group made up exclusively of black women, the older the better. It's my observation that they usually have especially good sense. But the really interesting thing about these ads is that the planning groups now have at least one fat guy as a member. I love it.

Okay, enough of that. A well-rounded meal, the kind that you'd serve when your in-laws come crashing in just at the time your wife is in the hospital with newborn twins, goes like this: a salad, some meat, vegetables, probably some kind of potatoes, maybe some bread, and usually a dessert. (All of this, by the way, is available at the local carry-out chicken place.) Let's go so far as to assume, however, that your mother-in-law's nose would be put seriously out of joint by anything but a homemade meal. Don't panic. Rise to the challenge.

We've already covered salads in our section on lunch, so you're partway home already. Two points: You can do the salads ahead of time and keep them in the fridge until it's time to eat. No, don't do the tossed-lettuce salad the day before. However, a half hour before is perfectly all right. Fruit salad can still look reasonably fresh for a couple of hours in the cooler; Jell-O or coleslaw can be done the day before. By the way, remember that Jell-O takes several hours to vulcanize. If you're planning to eat by six, better have the Jell-O in by two o'clock. I wouldn't do Jell-O and fruit salad at the same meal; throw the fruit *in* the Jell-O when you make it. Want to go the extra mile? Cut the Jell-O into reasonably sized rectangles and serve it on individual salad plates with a lettuce leaf. It's probably easier if you put the lettuce leaf on the salad plate and *then* put the Jell-O on top of that. Don't do this if you also plan to serve a tossed salad. Want to really pull out all the stops? Get a can of aerosol whipped cream and give each Jell-O square a shot just before it goes on the table. This adds nothing to the meal, but it's been shown to impress mothers-in-law.

Do not serve more than two salads at any one meal, unless you're hosting a group of maiden aunts. More than two salads will really piss off your father-in-law. We're seeking a nice balance here. One salad is plenty good enough, and a big tossed salad with lettuce, tomatoes, radishes, and stuff is the easiest to do. Let them scoop it up and dress it for themselves. This gives your guests a sense of participation, and the big salad bowl on the table takes up a lot of room and gives the impression of abundance. Also, you can save the leftovers this way. Important point: Don't just shove the salad bowl into the icebox or it will dry out and the lettuce will get brown around the edges. Instead, pack it into one of those Tupperware or Rubbermaid containers; the plastic bag that a new shirt comes in is an acceptable alternative, just be sure to staple up the open end.

One thing that nobody seems to want to talk about with dinner strategy, but perhaps we hinted at it above in our comments on the meaning of life: How badly do you want these people to come back? That is, do you really want to go all out for your sister and her darling kiddies, all of whom you love? Or would you really prefer to see these people keep on truckin' down the road? One of our family fables deals with my dear grandma, who served a group of moochers hot dogs three meals in a row before they got the message and moved on to the next stop.

As long as we've paused this long in what started out as a discussion, as you may recall, of the potato, let us comment just for a moment on this crucial point. We'll get back to feeding your in-laws (or, perhaps they in fact fall under this topic) all in due time:

▸ BAD FOOD

The way to move unwanted guests along is to feed them a meal that will motivate them to seek other quarters. This is especially important if you live somewhere that people want to be, such as Florida or California. My Aunt Elsie, who is a fine cook, never quite caught on to this concept. It seems that Cousin Otto's wife's sister lived in the same town. Guess where they crashed for a week at a time twice each year? Elsie, who is both a better cook and a better person than I am, never afflicted them with the anxious host's motivator: the All-White Meal.

Color, as you may realize, helps to make a meal appetizing. Thus, should you need to give unwanted guests a bit of a nudge, be sure that the meals are all one color, preferably white. (Now that I think of it, food that is all *blue* would work even better; however, you don't want to poison yourself.) Cooking smells help to add or detract from the joy of being a houseguest, and that's why we begin the All-White Meal with cauliflower. Boil up a big head of it and let it cook for a couple of hours until it's nice and mushy. This is a simple meal and requires no salad or dessert. Peel an appropriate amount of potatoes and boil them as well, only don't cook them for hours. About seven or eight minutes ought to do it just fine. Obtain a loaf of white bread from the day-old bread store and serve a stack of these wholesome slices; let the bread plate sit out on the table for at least an hour before the meal is to be served. Should you really have a mean streak, make up some instant tapioca (it's located in the section of the store where they have instant puddings and gelatin). Frozen fish sticks would be too obvious; serve frozen fish fillets, whatever's cheap (cod does nicely). After thawing the fish fillets, dip them in a little whipped egg and then some flour. Fry in hot fat for about ten minutes, only go much longer on one side than the other. Serve pale side up. Urge everyone to have seconds. Light up a cigar after dinner.

We'll not go on with this. By now you've realized that the combination of cauliflower, fried fish, and cigar smoke will ruin your own peace and comfort as the various odors swap about the house, combine, and fight it out for the next couple of days. You get the idea, though, and we don't need to go on about bad food. You've had plenty of it.

However, I'm not kidding about the essential points: Making a hit with the dinner you spread before your guests has to do not only with the obvious things like having food that tastes good and arrives more or less on time, but also with how appealing the performance is in terms of aroma and color. The Japanese have the right idea: Their food is supposed to look pretty. Fancy that.

So, we've looked at some fairly important concepts in terms of putting a meal on the table; we'll mention more on this as we go along. But for now, think about: (a) what you're going to serve and how it all balances out; (b) how long each thing is going to take to cook as you put together a schedule designed to have everything finish at about the same time; (c) how things are going to look and smell as well as taste; and, (d) what will please your guests most.

This last idea gets into a matter of style. My Aunt Annie (there were eight children in both my mother's and father's families; I've got *lots* of aunts) is a dear thing and we love her. She's also a fine cook. However, a meal at her house means that she's running back and forth, sweating to get things on, off, and cleaned up expeditiously; and the net result is a bunch of nervous diners who'd really rather have her sit still. It's hard to enjoy a meal while pots are being crashed about. Better she should have let the cleanup go until later. What may please your guests most is your companionship. Sit there and give it to them. Don't be hovering nervously between the kitchen and the dining room.

Enough of that. We began our discussion of dinner, you may recall, with comments on bread and potatoes. This is going on the assumption that you're planning to put on a traditional meal of meat, side dishes, bread, salad, dessert, and so on. Think about your audience. This kind of meal will be appropriate for lots of different crowds. It will impress the hell out of the new divorcee you've invited over ("I'm telling you, Gladys, the man's a perfect *dream*! He served homemade biscuits! He knows how to make gravy! And to think that I put up with that asshole Frank for so many years.") A traditional meal will wow the out-of-town relatives. Your boss's wife will think you're great, as will your wife's boss.

On the other hand, the guys in your poker club don't need this. You can't feed this to your wife and kids night after night without having to shop for your clothing at the fat boy's shop. The bean-sprout crowd from your dance class will let the mashed potatoes go to waste. Furthermore, the greater the complexity of your efforts, the further we have gotten from the principles of no-sweat cookery. Let us turn, then, to simple things that taste good and are easy to prepare: stuff you can turn to night after night that will please you if you're eating alone and will please the multitude if you're feeding a family.

▸ EASY STUFF

The great idea behind Easy Stuff is that there's *not* a lot of planning to go through. It's easy enough for just you, and it's easy enough for the softball team—just make more of it.

The true virtue of Easy Stuff is, of course, that it's ordinary. You can't live on caviar and lobster bisque night after night. Give me some potatoes. In the bakery we used to make beautiful petit fours. You'd gag if you ate more than two of them.

For some inexplicable reason, we have gotten away from the notion of "ordinary" as being a good thing. I honestly think of *ordinary* and *genuine* as being closely related. Maybe that's why I like Omaha. Multibillionaire Warren E. Buffett, who has more millions than Heinz has pickles, is listed in the phone book here. His tweed jacket could be described as nothing but ordinary. Nothing pretentious about this guy. Show me another *Fortune* cover feature as genuine. I see nothing at all wrong with "ordinary."

I will admit that while Easy Stuff is honest and genuine, it isn't beautiful. This is actually a virtue. Let me explain: Fancy food can be like fancy people, more trouble than it's worth.

I see a lot of students who are in midlife. Most of them are very interesting, intelligent people. I like them. Some of them I *love* (no, it's not what you're thinking; I keep my hands to myself; I'm no fool). However, there always is a certain percentage of insufferable little shits. I'm trying to be honest about this, and I trust that my outlook is not colored by the fact that I myself look like a Saint Bernard. (It's not *all* bad: Saint Bernards don't get messed with too often.) But the insufferable little shits—and there really aren't all that many of them—usually are among the formerly beautiful.

This compels me to elaborate on Thorson's Theory of Beauty: Beauty ruins a lot of people. They may tend to become self-centered and start to think that the reason they're fussed over is that they are in fact terrific people. Anyone who works on a tan for twenty summers in a row *will* wind up looking like an old saddle. And this is a sad thing indeed. The point inevitably comes where people either like you or dislike you because of who you *are,* not how you look. Old people know this, but it seemingly only begins to dawn on the middle-aged when they realize that nobody's making a fuss anymore. One might become bitter. It's possible to reach a point where it's too late to develop the personal qualities that the less gorgeous had to work on as teenagers in order to get along.

One that I remember in particular was joining the ranks of the formerly beautiful at about age forty-five. She just couldn't stand it, and as a result no one could stand *her.* She'd been the homecoming queen and the captain of the cheerleaders. She'd never worked on getting along with other people because she'd never *had* to. Now that she was no longer the center of attention, she was plenty mad about everything, looking for someone to blame.

So, if you're as ordinary as an Idaho potato, take consolation in the fact that you didn't peak too soon. Maybe you're easy to live with. Ordinary people and ordinary food, however, need not be dull. Here's some Easy Stuff that will bring beauty and excitement to your life:

High on the list of Easy Stuff is el quicko barbecue. This begins with meat that's already been cooked. Several days ago. It's still too good to throw away and it's yet to sprout moss. Every refrigerator has it: one leftover chicken breast, a couple of slices of roast beef, a few lumps of pot roast, one cold pork chop. The problem is endemic: You don't want to eat it, and you don't want to throw it away. Do this: Each time you've got some leftover meat that's perfectly good, *save* it. By saving it I don't mean just shoving that lone pork chop on a small plate and hiding it on the lower shelf. Wrap it in a piece of foil and freeze it. You'll accumulate a hoard after a while, so clean this out every so often before it takes over your freezer.

As you clean it out, make an appropriately sized pile, estimating how much you'll need for the evening meal. Just take enough of these little packages out of the freezer to take care of the needs that you'll anticipate. Take them out in the morning as you leave for work; they'll be thawed and ready to work with by the time you get home. Now, pay attention: *Do not* unwrap the little packages or peek in to see what's in each of them. This violates the rules of el quicko barbecue. Part of the glory of this is the surprise that's in store for you.

When you're ready to cook, unwrap your prizes and cut them up. Throw away the bones. Trim the fat off the ham. Make the pieces bite-size and prepare an amount appropriate to the number of mouths you're to feed: about one heaping handful each. Dump your chopped pieces of ham, chicken, beef, whatever into a large saucepan. Over this mélange pour enough bottled barbecue sauce to not quite cover the mess. Use whatever's handy; I like Hunt's Extra Thick and Zesty. Cover it, put it on low heat, and go on to better things. El quicko barbecue is ready as soon as everything is heated up throughout. It puts off a lovely aroma ("What's cooking? It smells *great*!") and is simplicity itself. Be sure to stir the blend as it heats.

You'll get both a good meal and the Calvinist satisfaction of salvaging good food that might otherwise have been thrown out.

El quicko barbecue is pretty brisk. It's Yang, so you'll want some Yin to go along with it: something dull to sort of take the edge off of the barbecue. Try idiot potatoes. Idiot potatoes come in two forms, both of which can be found in the freezer section of your local supermarket. Frozen French fries have gotten pretty good over the past few years. Buy them in the big bag for the sake of economy and just pour out however much you'll need, sealing up the remainder in the bag with one of those little wire twisters. Again, the rule of thumb is one handful for each person you're going to feed. (It occurs to me that some judgment is required here; if your hand is big enough to palm a basketball, it will hold more fries than your six-year-old daughter will eat.) You can either fry them or bake them. Frying them is a drag. It involves heating up a big frying pan with a couple of cups of oil in it, standing over the French fries and turning them while they're cooking, and then draining them on multiple pieces of paper towel. Try this instead: Arrange the still-frozen fries on a cookie sheet that's been lightly greased. (How to Grease a Cookie Sheet: Pour about a tablespoon of vegetable oil on the cookie sheet. Rub it around with a square of clean paper towel. It's easier to buy a Teflon cookie sheet.) Put this into a 400-degree oven for about ten minutes, or until they've turned light brown. Yes, this will give you French fries that are a bit dry. The alternative is French fries that are a bit greasy.

The other kind of idiot potatoes taste better and are just as easy: Tater Tots. In the store's freezer section, you'll now find, along with Tater Tots, all kinds of recently developed frozen potato products: hash browns, potato cakes, that sort of thing. Try a few different kinds. My observation is that the greater the relative surface area, the likelier they are to be crispy, a quality that's greatly desired with this kind of product. On the back of the package you'll invariably be given the option of frying or baking. Go with baking every time. It saves time and saves having to clean up a mess. Some will go so far as to give instructions for preparing the frozen-potato product via microwave. Ignore this.

El quicko barbecue and idiot potatoes make a fine meal. Add a green salad if you want to go the extra mile.

Idiot potatoes, obviously, go with lots of other things you can serve for dinner, foods we've already covered under the earlier section on lunch: grilled-cheese sandwiches, hamburgers, hot dogs, all kinds of sandwiches. Nosing about the kitchen-implement section of the store the other evening, I came across a French-fry cutter: a cross-hatched wire device that you apparently shove down on a potato to cut fries quickly. The wires, however, were about a half-inch apart, so you couldn't help but cut big, fat French fries with the thing. If the wires had been about a quarter of an inch apart, I'd have tried the thing in a scientific evaluation in our vast complex of test kitchens. However, I could see right away that the wide-wire approach had violated the Principle of Crunchiness. Like the little Tater Tots that have a lot of surface area relative to their volume, fries that are thin are crispy. Fries that are fat are all soft and mushy inside.

The Principle of Crunchiness isn't any scientific breakthrough. Why do grain elevators explode? Because grain dust has lots of surface area. You can't start a fire with a log and a match; you've got to split the thing up to increase the wood's surface area. This is easy enough, and it's the reason that you don't fry a whole potato: There's not enough *outside* to it—the inside is mushy and unappealing. As you increase size, surface area increases as a square of the length, but volume increases in proportion to the cube of the length. (Which is why, parenthetically, big knights couldn't wear full armor—it was too heavy for them to carry; a guy who was five foot four or less had a light enough suit that he could wear it and still stand up.) Based on measurement of old suits of armor, it was once maintained that nobody grew to be taller than five foot four in days of old. This was, of course, contrary to evidence from thousands of skeletal remains. However, I seem to recall that we were talking about crunchiness.

The obvious implication of the Principle of Crunchiness is this: If you *must* fry your fries and the idea of frozen French fries is anathema to you, then cut your fries so that they're *thin.* Remember how good McDonald's fries used to be? They used to run the whole potato through a cutter that made them nice and thin, thus crispy when cooked. I recall that they didn't bother to peel the potatoes, either; they just left the skins on. Try this. I would also urge you to buy one of those big, deep-fat fryers. *I'm* not going to that much trouble, but it's okay by me if *you* want to be a fussbudget about French fries.

Leftover French fries are, as you know, best fed to the hogs.

The Principle of Crunchiness serves us well for other things that are cut up: Little hunks are better than big hunks. This brings us to the next no-sweat meal: stir-fried stuff. It's kind of Chinese, but don't let that scare you.

Stir-fried stuff requires a sharp knife, a steady hand, and a frying pan (forget about buying a wok; that's only for the affected). Start with a likely looking onion and chop it into small pieces (not itsy-bitsy like you did for deviled eggs, just quarter-inch cubes will be fine). Do the same to a green pepper. Note that green peppers are filled at the factory with lots of white crud and seeds. You've got to get rid of this. Cut the pepper in half and then scoop the crud out with a teaspoon. Cut the pepper up just like you did the onion, then do the same to two or three stalks of celery. Then cut up some meat the same way. This works just fine with beef, pork, chicken, or shrimp. We seem to like the chicken best.

A few pointers on the meat: I cut up my stuff in the order given for a reason. The celery will take the onion and pepper odor off of your fingers, and I cut the meat last so that I only have to wash my knife and cutting board once. If, for some reason, I had cut the chicken first, I would really wash my hands, knife, and cutting board before going on and cutting up anything else. About a third of all chicken is shipped with some form of salmonella. This gets killed in the cooking process, but it lingers on cold things, such as cutting boards. It's been shown, by the way, that common liquid bleach kills the bacteria on the board just fine, whereas hot, soapy water just slows it down.

Okay, I'm a fussbudget; I've hit on this point several times and probably will again. There are instances, though, where being easygoing means compromising standards and making people sick. The First Law of No-Sweat Cookery is not to kill anyone.

A friend of ours heads the sanitation and restaurant inspection unit of the county health department. He recently took the family out to celebrate their son's college graduation. The whole crew got sick as dogs. Did *that* restaurant ever poison the wrong guy. There were inspectors crawling over the place the next morning. He tells me, by the way, that in addition to mishandling raw chicken, the most common disease spreader is the salad bar.

I think that the old guys who made sure everything was kosher were onto a good thing: It prevented lots of people from eating diseased pigs or bad oysters. I read recently that the infectious-disease folks at the Public Health Service have been kept hopping ever since sushi became popular. Raw meat has a lot of live bugs.

Peter Fruechen, the Danish explorer who lived for many years among the Greenland Eskimos, wrote of their need to be *agreeable.* As a result, they ate a lot of slop without protest. His thesis was that the demands of facing a harsh climate made it imperative for them to minimize interpersonal conflict. So if you'd ask one, "Is this the way to Thule?" he'd say that it was regardless of the truth of the matter. He didn't want to disappoint anyone.

Perhaps we've got it so soft that we go looking for trouble just for the excitement of it. Lord knows that finding somebody to blame has become a national pastime. If, however, you suspect that there's something gamy about the food you've been served, you'd *better* be disagreeable. Being a fussbudget about a clean cutting board is just fine by me.

Beef and pork, by the way, don't have anywhere near the bugs on them that chicken does; I'm still in the habit of cutting any meat last. A small piece of round steak or pork tenderloin works fine stir-fried. Shrimp is a little more trouble: I would cook the shrimp first, boiling it for about three minutes. Then cool and peel it, cut it up, and throw it into the stir-fry at the last minute. However, let's proceed with chicken.

Out of laziness, I've been buying the boned chicken breasts. When I was an undergraduate and had a lot more time than I had money, I'd never have *dreamed* of such an extravagance. On the other hand, that's when I was getting $2.25 an hour for changing truck tires. So it goes. At any rate, cut the chicken into strips, then cut the strips so that you've got pieces about an inch long and maybe a half-inch wide and thick.

In the meantime, have a couple of tablespoons of oil heating up in the frying pan on the stove's hottest setting. Start to sauté (a note to readers who just got stuck on that word: *Sauté* means to brown something in a frying pan) the chopped onion, pepper, and celery on high heat for a minute or so, stirring it up so that everything gets an equal chance. Toss in the meat and turn down the heat a little. If you've gone ahead and done this with beef or pork, it's going to take a little longer. However, if you're using chicken, frying it with the veggies on moderately high heat should take only three or four minutes. The chicken will first turn from pink to white, then to tan. It's done when the tan pieces start to get a little brown around the edges. I like to toss in some soy sauce at this point. This stuff goes great over rice.

Okay, I didn't tell you about the rice until now. Rice is so easy that it just slipped my mind. Minute Rice was given to us as a gift from one of the gods. Let's see if I can remember. No, Prometheus was the one who gave us fire. Well, nevertheless, boil a half cup of water each for however many persons you're feeding—four people: two cups. Toss in a pat of butter if you're trying to be fancy. As soon as the water boils, add the same amount of Minute Rice—two cups of rice to two cups of water for four people—turn off the heat, and put a cover on the pot. Do this just as you're starting the stir-fry and the rice will be done at the same time as the other goodies. Part of the pleasure of this meal is watching our youngest son, Pete, sort the celery out of his dinner. Pete considers celery to be poisonous. This is a great meal; serve it with more soy sauce.

Some random thoughts about poison, Koreans, and particulate matter: Koreans die of stomach cancer at a rate eight times higher than people in other nations and they eat an average of five pounds of soy sauce each annually. Is this cause and effect? I don't know. Maybe it's something else in the diet, or a genetic predisposition. Rotten food would do it. At any rate, we had a Korean couple as houseguests for a couple of weeks several years ago as part of a Friendship Force exchange, and we made the mistake of feeding them rare filet mignon. Lovely, prime Nebraska beef. No dice. Don't waste your time, should you have Korean houseguests, trying to get them to like rare beef. They were much happier with chicken soup, Rice-A-Roni, and fish. More like home. We also, in the spirit of sharing American traditions, put on a Thanksgiving turkey dinner, which they liked a lot. However, our oven wasn't any too clean, and the bird had spattered, so things got smoky in the kitchen and set off the smoke alarm out in the hall. It just about scared them to death.

I would speculate that, especially in the winter when houses are all closed up, cooking puts a lot of particulate matter into the atmosphere. Think of turning on the exhaust fan. Yes, I know that this defeats the purpose of all that insulation you've packed into the house. I'm reminded of the friend who's a virulent antismoker who thought to get back to the land and heat his house with a wood stove. He thus increased the particulate matter indoors by a factor of ten. There are some things that you don't want sealed in the house with you, and letting the smoke out every now and again might be a very good idea. In my business, gerontology, we talk about the free-radical theory of aging: By-products of oxidation or combustion may cause all sorts of problems, forming free radicals, which may be involved in the formation of cancerous tumors and other kinds of mischief. Thus, cigarette smoke isn't good for you. Neither is wood smoke, or turkey smoke, or the burned crust on your charbroiled steak. Products of oxidation, however ingested, may contribute to the generation of free radicals (defined by Alex Comfort as being like convention delegates: They'll combine with practically anything). They may well be related to the aging process itself.

Open the window a little; let the smoke out.

Let's continue, however, with more Easy Stuff, now that I've gotten you afraid to eat toast.

I really like these little hams that have a reduced salt content and claim to be 95 to 97 percent fat-free. Actually a lot of meat could be more fat-free; you just have to take the time to cut the fat off. Cooking a ham every now and again, though, is as easy as pie (actually it's *easier* than pie;

we'll cover pie later on); all you do is wrap it in foil and warm it up in the oven (325 degrees for forty-five minutes for one of the little two-pounders). This, however, inevitably leaves you with an inexact amount. Don't want to freeze the leftovers and dump it in the el quicko barbecue? Chop it up and dump it into a pot along with a can of Spanish rice. My dear old aged mother used to make Spanish rice from scratch, something that's become a lost art. I'd been using canned Spanish rice for years, not liking it too much because the kind I'd been buying was too bland, when I came upon La Preferida Spanish rice not long ago. Our store stocks it in the section with Mexican food. It's made by an outfit in Chicago called, you guessed it, La Preferida. This stuff is *great.* A can of it plus a cup of ham pieces makes a fine meal for three or four. My son Pete doesn't like it, so there's more for the rest of us. Bob, on the other hand, will eat anything, and usually does.

Something else you might want to try: stuffed peppers. The back of the La Preferida can (let's give these folks credit) recommends browning a pound of hamburger, draining off the grease, and combining it with a can of Spanish rice. Cut the white crud out of some green peppers and fill them up with this hamburger-rice mixture. Put them into a baking dish with a little water in it, cover it all with foil, and bake at 325 degrees for forty-five minutes. It occurs to me that you could also stuff the peppers with ham and Spanish rice. Sounds good.

While we're on the subject of peppers, I need to mention Sir Christopher Wren. His tomb is in the crypt at Saint Paul's in London. The Latin in the epitaph reads, roughly, "Do you seek his monument?" Well, then, *"lector, circumspece"* (reader, look about you). The whole magnificent cathedral that he designed serves as his monument. When you're looking over the bell peppers in the store, *circumspece,* look about you. You may have the great good fortune to find, right there among the green bell peppers, a few that are shaped the same but are bright red. *These peppers are perfectly good.* Seize one of them up, along with one of the green ones, and grab a medium-size onion while you're at it. Now head for the butcher counter in quest of Italian sausage.

The red bell peppers taste just the same as the green ones. I *swear* it. You want one of the red ones for the decorative value; the red will go nicely with the green and cheer things up. Sausage and peppers requires a little cheering up. Now, these are sweet peppers, not hot peppers. Telling them apart isn't hard. The sweet red peppers are exactly the same as the green ones, except for their color. The *hot* red peppers are long and thin, shaped kind of like an uncircumcised dick. You don't want these.

There is a rating scale, by the way, for the hotness of peppers. Bell peppers aren't even on the scale, as they're not at all hot. The scale, for some reason, goes from 0 up to 140, not from 0 to 100. The hottest peppers generally available in the United States are jalapeños, which rate a puny 40 on the scale. Tops at a rating of 140 are the Mombasa peppers, which are not used for food (except among the suicidal), but go into deep-heating muscle rubs and ointments.

Cut up the peppers and the onion, sauté in a little oil, add the sausage, and cover. Every now and again poke all up and down the sausage with a sharp knife; juice that's melted out of the thing will run out. Drain, serve with the peppers slopped over the sausage, and accompany with something light, such as Rice-A-Roni. Good eating.

I've mentioned Rice-A-Roni twice so far. Maybe you're not familiar with it. It's sold in stores in the—you guessed it—rice section, right next to Minute Rice. I'm not (unfortunately) getting paid anything by the manufacturers of these products, by the way (although I can be had cheap); they're actually the brands that I use. At any rate, Rice-A-Roni makes a dandy side dish, although you don't want to fix it if you're eating alone. One little box of the stuff makes enough to feed five or six, and I think that making a half box of it would be much more trouble than it's worth. Rice-A-Roni is a mixture of rice and macaroni (actually, vermicelli—literally, little worms—noodles cut to be about the same size as grains of rice), plus flavorings that you can toss in: chicken, beef, fried rice with almonds, Spanish. What you do is this: In a large frying pan that has a cover, brown the rice and macaroni in a little oil or margarine; after a few minutes you carefully pour in a couple of cups of water, add the seasoning powder, turn down the heat, and cover it. The steam at low heat makes the rice swell up, and in about fifteen minutes you've got a nice big mess of flavored rice. The vermicelli, which browns better than the rice, adds color and interest. Rice-A-Roni is one of the first of what has now developed into a string of side-dish products that includes various permutations of rice, varieties of noodles, different kinds of potatoes, and so on. All are useful for the bonehead cook. I like most of them a lot.

Rice-A-Roni is good with leftover meat, especially ham: Just as the stuff is nearing completion, starting to firm up and lose some of its watery quality, throw in a cup or two of chopped-up leftover ham. It doesn't seem to matter much whether you're using the chicken-flavored Rice-A-Roni or the beef-flavored; ham goes well with both. This is also a wonderful way to use up leftover turkey. Trim the used turkey well to get rid of all the gristle and little body parts, cut the big pieces down to bite size, and combine about two cups of the turkey pieces with one almost-finished load of chicken-flavored Rice-A-Roni. Cook for another few minutes, just long enough to warm up the meat. Not bad. This is a great thing to feed a brother-in-law who eats like a horse; it's cheap and there's plenty of it.

Are you stuck feeding a Cub Scout den and you've

discovered that there are only four hot dogs in the fridge? Cut them up into little pieces (the hot dogs, not the Cub Scouts), and add them to a potful of Rice-a-Roni. The kids *will* eat it.

One note about this stuff: The relative humidity in the kitchen will affect how well the rice absorbs the water. On a humid day it will take longer for the rice and vermicelli to soak up all the water. Thus it's possible to have everything else ready and find yourself stirring rice soup, cursing under your breath. This doesn't seem to happen so much in the winter when the air is dry in the house. A bit of advice: Go a little easy on the water (about one-quarter cup less) when the atmosphere is humid. Or, if you forget this, cook the stuff for the last six or eight minutes with the lid off the pan, so that more of the moisture evaporates. With this one caveat, Rice-A-Roni is really easy to fix; it's hard to screw this up unless you scorch it initially. So, watch it.

Not everything that comes out of a box, of course, is fit to eat. I'm trying to point out a number of products that I've found to be tasty and fairly easy to prepare. Sometimes you have to modify what you get, like throwing out half the powdered cheese that comes in the package of au gratin potatoes. Other times, though, there's just not much that can be done.

Lipton's Potatoes and Sauce, Chicken and Mushroom Flavor, is an example of a hopeless product. This is curious, as the other Lipton side dishes, particularly the rice dishes, are excellent. The chicken-and-mushroom-flavored instant potatoes, however, have that particular tang of industrial waste that many of us remember from the library paste they distributed when we were in the third grade. Elmer's glue was *such* an improvement when it came along.

As long as I'm warning the cautious consumer, there are a few other things to avoid if you would care to maintain your reputation. The Jimmy Dean sausage people put out a breakfast sausage that is, in my opinion, quite good. Unfortunately they took patties of this perfectly acceptable and very tasty sausage, put them between halves of biscuits made from Portland cement, and sealed them in transparent envelopes made from the plastic that goes into the construction of body bags. They purportedly are to be placed into a microwave oven in anticipation of an edible breakfast entrée. Printed on the box are several paragraphs of instructions suggesting a variety of ways to prepare this product in the fervent hope of making it less dismal and offensive. I've tried them all. They don't work. The person who developed this abomination should, in the words of Alexander Woollcott, be taken out and gently but firmly shot.

I have yet to find canned Chinese food that is fit to eat.

Armour Food Company, evidently feeling that the furor created by Upton Sinclair's *The Jungle* has all died down by now, has marketed what is laughingly called a breaded pork patty. Stamped out in the shape of a pork chop, they actually sell these things along with real food in the meat-counter section of the store, apparently trying to trick the unwary into the belief that they are acceptable for human consumption. They're not.

My friend Tony would drink nothing but Falstaff beer; being an employee of the company, he felt that he must be loyal. Would that Falstaff had been as loyal to him. They closed down their brewery here and fired everyone. Apropos of this, I was giving a talk not long ago about the genesis of the Pure Food and Drug laws, and I mentioned an anecdote from Sinclair's book about the packinghouse worker who fell into a vat and went out packaged as Swift's Pure Leaf Lard. Now, this is something that happened in about 1905, and I doubt that it was company policy even then. Nonetheless, several old ladies in the audience tut-tutted, reminding me that Swift and Company supported a generation of South Omaha slaughterhouse workers. This kind of whipped-dog subservience just drives me crazy. Should we hide bad news? Was there never a packinghouse that screwed its employees? Who should be loyal to whom?

Van de Kamps breaded fish, by the way, stinks. Too much bread, not enough fish. On the other hand, they have *great* commercials.

▸ FUNERAL CASSEROLE

As long as we're discussing one-dish meals, I need to share with you a taste from your childhood that you may have forgotten if life's gotten too sophisticated: funeral casserole. When Jean Shepherd speaks about his mother in her rump-sprung chenille bathrobe serving meat loaf and red cabbage, the memory takes him right back to Hammond, Indiana. Well, the thought of funeral casserole takes me right back to my boyhood in Northbrook, Illinois. My understanding is that in Minnesota this stuff is called tuna-noodle hot dish. I think of it as funeral casserole because all of the old ladies in our church kept a spare copy of it in the freezer, ready to pounce if someone died. In fact, it was quite possible for there to be several tuna-noodle casseroles at the house even before the news of the death had gotten around to the entire congregation. Some arrived before the corpse was cold. This has led me to theorize in later years that there must be some basic, biological need for this stuff among grieving people: The bereaved crave tuna fish.

A further comment before we discuss making this taste treat: When my father died, the thing that I remember with the most appreciation after all these years is Mrs. Fox from across the backyard, who sent over a big ham. I mean a *really* big one, all baked and laid out with pineapple slices. It fed the whole crew. Those well-meaning souls who brought funeral casserole got off for cheap, but they're not remembered after the passage of these many years. I also remember the lady across the street who came over after the funeral to see if there was anything we needed; she was nonplussed when I told her that in all actuality what was needed was more ice and another bottle of whiskey. She didn't come back. Let this be an object lesson: If you put yourself on the line by asking what they need, you'd better be willing to produce when they tell you. As a result, when I think it's appropriate, I bring a jug along, or, sometimes, a jug plus a couple of cases of beer. When you're thinking of meeting human needs, you might as well get right down to it and meet some.

Now, back to funeral casserole. Your kids deserve to eat some of this, if only as a part of their socialization to the culture. Who knows, they might develop a taste for it. I rather like creamed chipped beef on toast, which I know is quite an admission to make. (I don't, however, like it well enough to actually take the trouble to cook the stuff. Should you desire to find out the fixings for S.O.S., communicate with the army cooking school at Fort Lee, New Jersey. Cut down their recipe by a factor of four hundred.) Funeral casserole is pretty good, and it's economical. It can be stretched to feed a multitude if necessary.

Start with a medium-size package of egg noodles. These things come in two sizes: medium and huge. The medium bag will do. Cooking for three or four? Use half the package of noodles. Cooking for six or more? Use the whole thing. Poor people? Use the huge bag, only have a bully-big baking dish ready, because all the noodles won't fit into a regular dish. Now, here's the rub: *You've got to cook the noodles first.* There's just no way out of it. Throwing the dry, uncooked noodles together with the rest of the stuff and baking it will give you starch casserole. There's an art to cooking noodles, and this goes for the regular, flat, egg noodles used in this dish as well as for macaroni and spaghetti noodles. Get the water hot first. For half a pack of egg noodles, two quarts of water in a saucepan is enough; for a full package of egg noodles or for spaghetti, use a big pot, such as a Dutch oven, with at least four inches of water in it. Remember, the water will boil more quickly if you: (a) use hot tap water to start with; and (b) put a lid on the pot while it heats. As soon as the water boils, throw in the noodles, turn the heat down to medium, and cover. In the meantime, find the colander and get the dirty dishes out of the sink. Keep an eye on the noodles to see that they don't boil over. Give them a poke every now and again. While this is happening, open a regulation-size can of tuna and use the lid to keep the fish inside the can while you turn it over in the sink and then squeeze the oil (or water) out. This will squash the tuna all together, so you'll have to pick it out of the can with a fork when the time comes. Remember this.

After the noodles have boiled for about eight minutes, drain them in the colander in the sink. Now: *Wash the noodles in the colander with hot tap water.* This is a key to cooking success that they never tell you about in the fancy cookbooks. For some reason, other authors think that you're born with this knowledge. I know better. I was once served spaghetti by a well-meaning girl who hadn't rinsed her noodles; they stuck together like glue. Pick up the colander and sort of swish it around as the hot water pours over the just-cooked noodles. Give it a good one. Turn off the water and shake the excess water out of the thing. Shake it like hell; this goes double for spaghetti. The last thing you want is watery spaghetti. Dump the cooked, rinsed, and shaken noodles into a baking dish. Fork the tuna in on top of them. Pour in a can of concentrated cream of mushroom soup. Fill this same can about halfway with milk, swishing it around to get the rest of the soup unstuck from the side of the can. Add it and stir up everything with vigor. A matter of philosophy here: Judy says to blend the concentrated mushroom soup and the half can of milk in a saucepan on the stove before heaving it into the baking dish on top of the tuna and noodles. Judy maintains that this keeps you from having to break up big clots of the congealed soup. Doing this, I think, violates the spirit of no-sweat cookery: It adds one step and dirties a pot that you then have to wash. Just throw it all together and stir it up with gay abandon; let the clots fall where they may. Now, for the *pièce de résistance:* Crumble eight or ten potato chips over the top. Pop this sucker into a 325-degree oven for forty-five minutes; serve it right in the baking dish, being careful to put a hot pad on the table first. Keep a sharp eye on the first kid who helps himself: Some will use the strategy of scraping the top with the serving spoon before digging in, thus garnering all of the toasted potato chips for his own serving. Deal sternly with this cupidity.

The principle one must hold close to one's heart is, of course, this: You *must* always rinse the noodles. This goes for all kinds: flat, spaghetti, macaroni, you name it. By this sign are real cooks differentiated from screw-ups. Noodles that have not been rinsed will be immediately apparent to all, causing regret and embarrassment; they stick together and taste starchy. Don't let this happen to you. Should you find a stickiness problem among your noodles even after a conscientious rinsing, stir a teaspoon or two of vegetable oil among the noodles. This should not be necessary; consider it a fallback position, only to be used in dire circumstances.

Once the noodle-rinse-and-shake procedure is mastered, one can proceed to other uses of pasta. Remember, the noodle is our friend. Manufacturers have been making friends among a gratified public in recent years by selling decorator noodles. Many a bland and dreary January day has been pepped up with curlicue noodles in multiple colors: basic yellow, plus both orange and green. There are some exotic applications for decorator noodles. You may wish to go back and review our earlier comments on macaroni salad. A basic tuna or chicken salad can be stretched to an almost unlimited degree by adding these little cuties (they still have to be cooked, rinsed, and excess water shaken off them, remember; for salads, they must also be *cooled*). The smart set, in fact, has gone nuts over cold pasta, being apparently under the mistaken impression that it's not as fattening as any other carbohydrate. This is, of course, absurd. Want to diet and actually lose weight? Cut out bread, potatoes, desserts, and pasta. Want to be stylish? Eat decorator noodles.

But let us say a word or two more about good old flat egg noodles. Just plain noodles substitute nicely as a side dish in place of potatoes when you're serving something that has a little gravy to pour over them. Pot roast comes to mind. However, noodles fall flat just by themselves if there's nothing else in the meal to jazz them up. I notice that several companies are putting out noodle side dishes that are packaged in foil envelopes. Typically, they require only that the contents be boiled for eight minutes or so with a couple of cups of water and milk plus a dab of margarine. I've tried several, and they're pretty good. Lipton's noodles Alfredo are first-rate. This is an easy side dish with most meat dishes. I keep a couple of packages around for meals that are essentially unplanned. In other words, this stuff is good if you're throwing something on the table at the last minute, which I seem to be doing about half the time. I note that these noodles don't need to be rinsed. I presume that either they've already been rinsed at the factory or else the powdered sauce is so strong as to overwhelm any starchy flavor that the noodles might have. At any rate, they don't taste like library paste, and they're a handy alternative to potatoes.

So is stuffing mix. I'm not talking here about the Pepperidge Farm stuffing that goes into a turkey—more on that later. I mean Stove Top, a prepackaged side dish that comes in a red box (or green for "pork" flavored, and so on). I can't tell much difference between them; take your pick. However, don't fall for the so-called gourmet stuffing mix that costs twice as much as the other kind (it contains a few freeze-dried mushrooms); it's not as good as the cheaper stuff. Fixing stuffing mix is *really* easy: Just heat up some water, add a little margarine, add the envelope of spices when the water boils, and add the envelope of bread crumbs a minute or two later. Turn off the heat and put a lid on it. It's ready in five minutes. Flake it up a little with a fork as you dig it out of the pot. This goes especially well with pork chops or fried chicken.

Speaking of easy—I almost hate to bring this up—Hamburger Helper Chili with Beans (just add browned hamburger) is *excellent.* Really. Chili, like barbecue, is one of those dishes that men who can't cook think they can cook. I've had some truly wretched chili over the years; too hot, too bland, too greasy, you name it. The Hamburger Helper product seemingly strikes the right balance. Just brown and thoroughly drain a pound of hamburger in a large frying pan that has a cover. Be sure to get all the grease off. Add the stuff from the package and some water, following the directions on the box. Then turn down the heat, cover, and simmer. Make in any multiples that you need; one package serves from four to six adults. Serve by itself with crackers, or in smaller portions as a prelude of things to come, such as hot dogs and potato salad.

Now, don't get me wrong: It's all right to be persnickety about your personal chili recipe if you've got a good one. Hamburger Helper Chili with Beans is an acceptable alternative (unlike most canned chili, which is vile) if you're in a hurry.

Moving right along with idiot side dishes: The prepackaged macaroni and cheese has gotten pretty good. In most cases the dry noodles have to be cooked and rinsed, combined in a pot with some powdered cheese and a little milk, and then reheated until the powdered cheese melts into the noodles. While this may seem burdensome, you're paying for greater convenience with the other side dishes; you have to work a little more with this stuff because it's really *cheap.* Go for the store's brand. It's not too good, but maybe you're trying to feed a mob and you're broke. Or do they deserve better?

Top of the line among packaged macaroni-and-cheese products is Velveeta Shells and Cheese Dinner. It's *cheesier* than the cheaper varieties. Perhaps this is because it contains a little foil envelope of cheese rather than the powdered stuff. To me, powdered instant cheese has kind of an overbearing flavor. The Velveeta brand seems to strike a nice blend of cheese taste that's both mellow and piquant yet not pushy. It's made pretty much the same way as the other products: Boil and rinse the noodles, drain, put them back in the pot and add the cheese. It's best to actually *time* the noodles when cooking: about ten minutes. Then test one of them; bite into it. A tough, undercooked macaroni noodle is an abomination before the Lord. They've made adding the cheese easy: Just squeeze the foil envelope. One used to have to go around a little can with a rubber spatula in an attempt to get the last bit out. Mixing the cheese with the noodles is, theoretically, the last thing that needs doing and then you are ready to go. But not quite.

Here comes another of those how-to-do-it tips that has made this book *well* worth its purchase price to you. The makers of Velveeta Shells and Cheese Dinner obviously never considered the mess that could be made or the sorry results achieved by trying to stir up a can of cold cheese with a pot full of hot, wet noodles. If you just beat the hell out of it, you'll break up all your macaroni into little bits that look like they've been through a blender. If you go to it tenderly, there will be big gouts of unmelted cheese lurking about in your macaroni.

There are two strategies you can use, both of which work well. Either put the stuff in a pot over low heat or put the noodles and cheese together into the serving dish. Next, in both cases, take two regular knives—I'm talking flatware here, not sharp kitchen knives—and form them into the shape of an X with their points down. Then stick them into the noodles and cheese and make a scissorslike motion, rubbing each blade against the other as you draw them closed and open, going all through the noodles and breaking up the cheese. (A note for our more advanced pupils: This is the same technique used in breaking up the shortening in homemade pie dough, a topic that will not be covered further in this book.) If you've done this on the stove, the combination of the scissoring motion and the low heat will melt and combine the cheese nicely. However, you've now got a cheesy pot to clean. If you have a microwave oven, better to scissor the cheese into the noodles right in the serving dish (plan ahead: Don't use a metal dish), then microwave the stuff for a minute or so, which will put some heat back into it and melt the little blots of cheese that are left. Stir it a wee bit more with a spoon, then serve it to a grateful public.

Macaroni and cheese goes down particularly well with kids, especially with little kids who may not have very sophisticated tastes. Finicky eaters will usually put down some macaroni and cheese. It's also nice and mild as something to serve to give the family nourishment after the stomach flu has swept through your household. Jell-O and tea and toast are old reliables as well.

A word about barf: While keeping things in the kitchen scrupulously clean will help to prevent poisoning your family, inevitably someone is going to bring home a bug from school or your teenager is going to come home with a snootful. Anybody with kids has to cope with a certain amount of vomit over time. Thus we see child rearing as the ultimate in delayed gratification. Research in my field has shown that childless old people as a rule don't do nearly so well as those who have had children. In the meantime, however, somebody's going to have to clean up the puke. Knowing this, our first set of furniture was black vinyl. Easy to wipe off without staining.

However, the kid will just naturally aim for the rug. He'll really *mean* to get to the john in time, but sooner or later you'll have to clean barf out of a rug. Here's what you do: For starts, you want to get rid of the smell *right now* so you're not barfing yourself. Sprinkle the warm puddle with a couple of ounces of rubbing alcohol. Really. Plain old isopropyl rubbing alcohol. It masks the odor nicely so that you can get down to business. This is something you want to get up quickly, so don't fart around looking for a mop. Grab a couple of old turkish bath towels. Get the big hunks up with a dry one, then go over the patch with one that you've wrung out in hot water. This may be all that's necessary. Let's assume, though, that we're involved in a serious case here. The next step is to go over the place with a scrub brush and about two ounces of household ammonia in a gallon or so of hot water. This should pretty well defeat the smell, but you should also go back over this again with warm suds—dishwashing soap will do. If you've saturated the rug by now, a Shop-Vac is invaluable for pulling water out of a rug. The whole idea is to work fast before things have a chance to soak through entirely. We had an affliction, though, of one nineteen-year-old son cutting loose at four in the morning with a combination of beer, black Russians, and cucumber sandwiches. Things being the way they were, proper cleaning didn't start for several hours.

Now, Dartmouth psychiatrist George Vaillant speaks

of *suppression* as one of the truly mature adaptive mechanisms (this is as differentiated from *repression,* a seemingly inexplicable failure to acknowledge something unpleasant). Suppression is deliberately postponing emotional violence, employing a stiff upper lip, planning to deal with something later. Yes, things are in a hell of a mess, but I don't have time to wring hands and whine right now; somebody had damn well get the baby out of the burning house. Suppression is what gets the work of the world done, even if we *do* feel a bit cranky.

And suppression is what we hope you'll employ when *your* teenager deposits a stomachful of beer, black Russians, and cucumber sandwiches on your blue shag rug in the middle of the night. Yes, it would be nice to just call time out and give the little bastard a new crack in his ass. However, worry about that later. Somebody's got to clean up the barf and be quick about it.

Should things still stink to high heaven even after the ammonia wash (they did), try this: Get up as much of the moisture as is humanly possible. If you don't have a Shop-Vac or wet-dry vacuum cleaner, *rent* one (have the decency to clean it out after you've used it). Then put down *lots* of paper towels and walk around on them, pressing the paper towels down hard so that they absorb as much as possible. Repeat as often as necessary. Further dry the carpet by setting a fan to blow on it overnight. When it is completely dry (you'll have to *touch* it to find out, you big sissy), get some Carpet Fresh. This is a powdered product made by Airwick; my preference is for the green container ("Fragrance II") which is supposed to have the blend that eliminates pet odors (I'd like to see it get a dog-piss stain out of a hardwood floor). Having tried several other products, I'm here to tell you that this stuff *works.* Sprinkle the powder over the parameters of the unfortunate incident, let it sit there overnight, and then vacuum up the powder the next day. Fresh as the proverbial daisy. Now go put itching powder in your son's jockstrap.

Where was I? Ah, macaroni. Macaroni and cheese is another of these wonderful things that can serve as a main dish as well as a side dish. Cut up some ham in it, cut up some hot dogs in it, you know how we work by now.

Packaged instant potatoes work the same way. Au gratin instant potatoes are all pretty much alike, so go for the store brand. There are other varieties and flavors; try several kinds and see what you like. They work pretty much the same way as the noodle mixes, only with even *less* effort, if that's possible. Heat up the amount of water that's called for, along with a little milk and some margarine, and combine in a flat baking dish with the contents of the package. A tip here: The powdered cheese is just as overpowering with the au gratin potatoes as with the packaged macaroni and cheese. What to do? Throw half of it away, that's what to do. Experiment a little and see if you agree with me. I use all of the potatoes and water and milk, but I've found that there's, let us say, an overly generous portion of the powdered cheese, so I only use half of it. This dish bakes for forty-five minutes and is also another good hiding place for used ham.

Let's say that you want to pull out all the stops and not rely on packaged, freeze-dried potatoes (they are, I'll admit, an acquired taste). Here's how we do au gratin potatoes with *real* potatoes: Start with a baking dish about thirteen inches square that has a cover. Peel four or five likely looking potatoes and slice them fairly thin (about three-sixteenths of an inch or a little less). Slice enough potatoes to cover the bottom of the baking dish about an inch deep. This was just a measure of volume; scoop back up about half of the sliced potatoes now. Slice about six nice, thick slices of cheese (it has to be yellow cheese in this instance; that's the law). I suppose one could use

Cheddar or Colby for this, but I wouldn't. Velveeta is just fine for this. Arrange the cheese slices over the bottom layer of sliced potatoes, then lay down the rest of the spuds. Put two cups of milk in a blender along with about four pats of margarine, a teaspoon of onion salt (you'll have to take the little plastic shaker thing off in order to get your spoon in there; you're allowed to do this), and a heaping tablespoonful of *cornstarch.* You remember cornstarch. Right, the yellow box with the Indian maiden growing out of an ear of corn. Mom had some on the shelf. Well, it's still available: Argo cornstarch, in the grocery section with the baking goods. It's the basic stuff for thickening sauces and gravies, and we'll call upon it again. Blend the milk, margarine, onion salt, and cornstarch together, then pour it over the potatoes and the cheese. Use just enough to not quite cover all the potatoes. Put the lid on the baking dish and bake in a 350-degree oven for about forty minutes. Take the lid off and turn down the heat a little if this stuff starts to boil over in the oven. You want a brown (not a black) crust on the top when it's done. If for some reason things are looking pretty pale still after forty minutes, take the lid off and keep on baking for another five or six minutes. Again, chunks of ham go nicely in this dish. I like this combination better than ham and scalloped potatoes; the cheese makes it more interesting. Be sure to put a hot pad on the table.

So far, we've been talking about side dishes that can also serve as main dishes, or one-dish meals. Spaghetti falls into this category, although when I serve it, I always serve it as a main dish. The steak houses in Omaha for some reason all serve a little bowl of spaghetti along with a steak. The interesting thing is, this is almost always really *bad* spaghetti, while the steaks one gets here are usually excellent. Perhaps they pay more attention to the spaghetti that's meant to be a main dish. Spaghetti can be the centerpiece of a really substantial, even a memorable, meal. Tourists take note: Should you be in Omaha on a Thursday in any of the months from September through May, take pains to get yourself at lunchtime down to the Sons of Italy Lodge, 1238 South 10th Street, for a phenomenon that's as interesting sociologically as it is gastronomically. The members of the Lodge, or at least the retired guys, serve a spaghetti lunch to all comers (and about nine hundred to a thousand show up each Thursday) as a fundraising project. It's interesting to see fifty or sixty short, fat guys screaming at each other in the kitchen, but they also serve the best homemade spaghetti *I've* ever had. I won't say that it's the best in the world, but it's hands-down better than the stuff I've sampled in Little Italy in Manhattan and other places where you'd think they know how to cook spaghetti. These old guys work a rotation, so one week they'll serve spaghetti and meatballs, the next it will be spaghetti and homemade Italian sausage, next will be mostaccioli and so on. On great occasions (as, for example, the Thursday before Christmas) they'll have a dish they call Marco Polo: spaghetti with beef tips.

These guys make their sauce by the barrel; they start the day before, and they take their task seriously. I'm not going to tell you how they do it because quite frankly I don't know, although these are good old guys and they'd share their recipe with me if I asked for it. Knowing, however, that I can get a plateful of pure bliss once a week for only $4, I don't go to the trouble of making homemade sauce. I don't try to paint the Mona Lisa over again, either. It seems to me that the kind of guy who would take the time to do homemade spaghetti sauce isn't the person who's really interested in no-sweat cookery. There are easier ways to live.

Unfortunately, making a good meat sauce for your spaghetti using off-the-shelf sauce isn't entirely effortless, either. Bear with me, though, it's worth the trouble.

First, find by experimentation what kind of sauce you like. I personally prefer Ragu' Thick & Hearty type. Paul Newman puts out a variety that he calls Industrial Strength, which is anything but; however, it's not bad if you like a mild, light sauce. I like a little more strength to mine. Also, don't be fooled into thinking you can just dump this stuff over a pile of cooked noodles. Here's what you do: Chop up and sauté a medium-size onion. Open up a little can of mushroom stems and pieces, *drain* them—pour off the fluid that they were canned in—and dump them in with the onions. Cook until the edges of the onion pieces start to brown a little, and then add a pound of hamburger, crumbling it with your fingers as you put it into the frying pan. Brown the hamburger over medium heat. About midway into the process of browning the hamburger, sprinkle over it a goodly portion (at least a teaspoon) of *coarse* black pepper. It's not necessary to grind your own; I'm constantly amazed at the people who couldn't find their ass with both hands who have the temerity to be snotty about their pepper. On the other hand, the finely ground stuff loses its punch. They sell coarsely ground black pepper in the spice section of the store. Continue browning the hamburger-onion-mushroom blend until all of the pink is cooked out of the meat, then drain off as much of the grease as possible. Come on, you can do better than that.

Meanwhile, back at the ranch, you should be starting to cook your noodles. I think the thinner ones, like vermicelli, are better, probably because they're less likely to taste starchy. At any rate, cook the noodles the same way we cook macaroni noodles, being careful to rinse them afterward and then to *drain* them especially well—you don't want water seeping out to the edge of your plate while you're eating spaghetti.

Add the jar of sauce to your cooked and drained hamburger-onion-mushroom mix. At this point there's something that I've just *got* to do; my Calvinist upbringing demands it. I take the jar after I've poured out the sauce and put about an ounce of hot water in it, then put the lid back on and shake it like mad, thus getting all the rest of the sauce that's been clinging to the bottom and the sides of the jar into suspension; then I dump it in with the rest. Such is the neurotic behavior of those of us who were socialized into the clean-plate club. Put this on medium heat, covered, and stir it every now and again to keep it from scorching on the bottom of the pan. Be careful with this stuff as it cooks, since it will splash out little droplets of hot sauce as it starts to boil, not unlike the boiling mudflats at Yellowstone National Park. Turn down the heat at this point to a low setting.

Making sure that the noodles are drained particularly well, dish this stuff onto the plates in the kitchen; serving it any other way will be a colossal mess. It's permissible to find out how big a load each of the eager diners plans to devour and then to dish it up accordingly. I personally go light on the noodles and heavy on the sauce. This goes great with a green salad; nothing else is needed with this meal. Want to go the extra mile? Serve this over one or two cooked Italian sausages. Judy and I are in agreement that Hillshire Farm mild Italian sausage is first-rate. I've heard of hot-sausage people who are somehow able to maintain a marriage with mild-sausage people, but I can't imagine how. Despite my grumpiness and her long-windedness, we are able to overlook each other's petty shortcomings and look forward to the approaching golden years, happy in the knowledge that we will walk hand in hand as two mild-sausage people. Want to make a completely different taste? Chop up a green bell pepper along with your onion and sauté it before adding the hamburger. Or, substitute bulk Italian sausage for the hamburger (be prepared to drain off massive amounts of grease). If you're feeding lumberjacks in the wintertime, add garlic bread to this meal. Get a loaf of unsliced French bread and cut it into thick slices—say, an inch and a quarter thick. Take a stick of margarine and put it into a little Corning Ware baking dish, then microwave it for sixty seconds until it's entirely melted. Add about half a teaspoon of garlic powder to the melted margarine and stir it up. Then paint one side of each bread slice, using a pastry brush. A pastry brush is one of those little brushes with white bristles that they sell in the kitchen-gadget section; it's also useful for putting barbecue sauce on chicken. Don't have one of these handy? A one-inch paintbrush will work equally well (be sure it doesn't smell of turpentine). Wrap the bread slices in a large piece of foil and put them into a 350-degree oven for about eight minutes. Plan on two slices of garlic bread per victim.

When I grew up in Chicago right after the war, I remember that my mother had this really wicked-looking bread knife with a serrated blade and a little wire guide that sat parallel to the blade, which I suppose was there to help you gauge the thickness of the bread slice. All the bread we got from the store was already sliced, so I asked her why she had the thing, and she told me that none of the bread sold during the war was sliced. It seems that the idea was that bread crumbs wouldn't go to waste if you sliced your own bread. Right. What's the natural thing to do with the few crumbs left after you slice a piece of bread? You give them the old heave-ho, of course. I recall when I worked at the bakery that they *did* save the bread crumbs there. Every so often they got swept into a big leftover-sugar bag (I'm talking one hundred pounds of sugar; this was a substantial bag). As they'd fill up, they'd be set aside and a farmer would come pick them up every few weeks; he'd feed the bread crumbs to his hogs. Big commercial bread bakeries would have even more reason to save the large amounts of bread crumbs that they'd generate by slicing thousands of loaves. Was there a bread crumb shortage during the war? Of course not. I should think that the steel that went into making all of those bread knives would potentially have been a likelier shortage. Oh well, there were no doubt even greater contributions to the war effort that were thought up by various pinheads. We had blackout shades in the schools at that time, too. Not that the school was ever lit up at night. Still, I'm sure a lot of Japanese bombers missed Chicago altogether because of the blackout shades in the Thomas Coonley School.

Once you've mastered the art of cooking the spaghetti noodle, a host of other one-dish meals are open to you. Here's one that's really easy and is also a good way to get rid of those last little shards of leftover turkey that are too big to throw away: Sort of Turkey Tetrazzini. This is called Sort of Turkey Tetrazzini not because you use sort-of turkey, but because the dish is a sort-of tetrazzini. To feed three or four people, start with about half a package of spaghetti noodles; cook them up just as we've already described. After draining them, dump them back into a saucepan, add about two cups of turkey pieces and a can of Cheddar cheese soup. Add a little hot water to the empty soup can and sort of swish it around to get the last bit of goody; add it, but don't go nuts on the water, this stuff gets drooly pretty fast. Add a full tablespoon of Worcestershire sauce. Now stir it all up on medium heat until it's evenly blended and heated up. You're done. Simple.

You will note in this section on Easy Stuff that it's possible to make substitutions, use different kinds of leftovers, and be creative in various ways. Pieces of ham, chicken, and leftover roast beef often go well mixed in with the flavored rice or noodle dishes. There are some things that *don't* go together, too, and you'll find out as you experiment what seems to work and what doesn't. Tuna doesn't work when mixed in with macaroni and cheese, for example; we tried it the other night and found that out. Putter about, though, and learn by doing.

▸ VEGGIES

Vegetables are sort of a transition, as I see it, between the easy one-course meals and sure-enough main dishes. We've already covered potatoes and baked beans pretty well. And there are some vegetables, such as turnips and beets, that nobody will eat no matter how they're prepared, so this section will be necessarily brief.

One has to view vegetables in the proper light. For years you've been told to finish your vegetables, that vegetables are good for you, that vegetables are full of vitamins. Vegetables have taken a bad rap. Veggies are there: (a) to add some color to the meal; (b) to provide some variety; and (c) to please your mother. A few are there because they taste good.

I just love these people who get worked up over things that in fact have no real meaning, like: *When you pour off the water the vegetables have been cooked in, you're throwing away most of the vitamins!* They're always so terribly earnest when they say this. Does anybody really *give* a shit? Okay, *don't* cook your vegetables. *I* don't care. *Save* the water that they're cooked in. It's all right by me. Keep a jug of it in the garage. Store it up in case there's a shortage. Whip up a nice mess of Jerusalem artichokes and bottle the juice; tell the neighbors about it. Gargle with the damn stuff.

I had to get that out of my system. Let me say just a few more offensive things and I'll be done. My secretary says that she knows a good way to cook rhubarb. I doubt it. When we were in Georgia, people said that okra was pretty good. I wouldn't know. I have known many who claim to have a good recipe for squash. They've got to be kidding. It is said that a hostess once offered Babe Ruth some asparagus; he declined, saying, "It makes my urine smell." Everyone who has a home garden wants to give away the zucchini. That's because they can't stand it either.

On the other hand, fresh corn on the cob is manna from heaven, and where would corned beef be without cabbage? There is something to be said for the vegetable; just don't get pushy.

For those who consider veggies to be a necessary evil, the less said the better: Stick with Green Giant. Pick out the type of vegetable that offends you the least from the frozen food section. Poke a hole in the plastic bag. Microwave it for six minutes. You're done. Don't have a microwave oven? Boil the bag—with no holes in it—for fifteen minutes.

Do you actually like vegetables? Then give them a little pizzazz. This may be difficult to imagine, but stick with me for a moment. Cooked carrots can be pretty good, provided they're swimming in melted butter. Or, try this: Peel and cook up a mess of carrots, cut into about two-inch pieces. Bisect the thick parts. Boil in not very much water until they start to yield when you stick a fork into them. Drain off *all* the water (send it to your sister-in-law if you wish), put the cooked carrots into a serving bowl, and pour about three tablespoons of lemon-flavored salad dressing over them. Oriental Chef Creamy Lemon salad dressing is now available in the store. It's *great.* Watch it if you keep your salad dressing in the fridge like I do; you may need to microwave the carrots and dressing for about forty-five seconds right before serving.

Judy and I were VISTA volunteers in North Carolina back in the sixties. Do you remember hearing about "outside agitators"? That was us. We learned a number of things at that time, much of which was an appreciation for Southern-style cooking. Black friends introduced us to sweet potato pie. Wonderful stuff. It gave me a renewed respect for the sweet potato. Quickie sweet potatoes go nicely with fried chicken. Here's how: Don't bother getting the raw ones; buy a can of yams. Pour off the juice that they've been canned in and put them in a baking dish. Now place three pats of margarine on top of them and pour about two ounces of maple syrup over the top. Bake for only about fifteen minutes in a 350-degree oven. Beauty.

The green pea is a humble vegetable, and one that is hard to love. Canned peas just don't cut it, in my opinion. However, green peas with pearl onions (available in the frozen food section) are not bad at all.

You know how good raw broccoli and cauliflower pieces are when served with onion dip as hors d'oeuvres. There's no law that says that you can't serve them to your kids this way at dinnertime. Many veggies are better raw than cooked. Should you really *have* to cook broccoli or cauliflower, don't go overboard. Drain it thoroughly after cooking and pour a little melted Cheez Whiz over the top. Should you be melting your Cheez Whiz in the microwave, remember to stop midway and stir it up so that it has a uniform texture throughout.

My friend Leo is from Belgium, and he tells me that the brussels sprout is unknown in Brussels. Similarly, the French fry is not generally available in France (ask for *frites* should you want some, and don't be surprised if they're served with vinegar). Green Giant frozen brussels sprouts are easy to deal with: Just boil that old pouch. Fresh ones are now, unfortunately, a rarity in many stores. If you find some, figure on about five per person who will actually eat them; boil them lightly and put a few pats of real butter on top just before you serve them. Or try this: Put some crumbled-up bits of bacon on top of the butter.

Cooked cabbage goes nicely with Polish sausage as well as with corned beef. Cut the head of cabbage into quarters. Put them into a large saucepan with about an inch of water and sort of steam it on fairly low heat for about fifteen minutes. The cabbage will get pale and tender as it cooks; don't go so long as to make it mushy. Put a pat of margarine on each piece when you serve it. Kraut is best straight out of the can; just heat it up in its own juice; pour off the juice when you serve it.

Canned corn is not worth bothering with. I'll stick with good old Green Giant Niblets in butter sauce nine times out of ten; it actually tastes like corn. Fresh sweet corn is wonderful if it's actually fresh; our stores here in Nebraska all have sweet corn all winter long, and it's the *formerly* fresh variety. Getting corn in Nebraska that's been shipped in from Florida seems strange somehow. During the season we'll have guys in parking lots selling the real stuff out of the back of pickup trucks. They are the true servants of mankind.

Shucking sweet corn is an important process, not to be taken lightly. One must remove *every* piece of corn silk fastidiously. Fill a Dutch oven or other big pot about four or five inches deep with hot water and get the water boiling before you put the corn in. Then boil it for exactly seven minutes, no more, no less. It is said that Mrs. Florenz Ziegfeld boiled the corn until the cobs were soft; you don't want to do this. Serve with real butter.

Green beans are, to me, the most versatile of vegetables, and the least offensive. A quick casserole based on the green bean: Take two regulation-size cans, drain off the juice they've been packed in, and dump them into a baking dish. Pour in one can of golden mushroom soup. Top with some of the canned French-fried onions. Bake for about thirty minutes in a medium oven (about 350 degrees or so). This is something worthwhile to take to a covered-dish supper at church if you're really cheap.

Judy likes fresh green beans cooked so little that

they're hot but still crunchy. If you've got some fresh ones, lop the ends off and cut the beans in half; wash them. Put into a pot with an inch of water, a pat of margarine, a tablespoon of white vinegar, about a half teaspoon of salt, and about a half teaspoon of coarse black pepper. Heat to boiling, cover, and turn the heat down to low; cook for less than ten minutes. I like mine Southern style, and cooking them this way relieves you from the obligation of using fresh beans: Canned are cheaper and less work. Drain off the juice in the can and then fill the canful of beans up again with water; dump this into a saucepan. Half-fry two pieces of bacon; when it's starting to brown, dump the bacon and the bacon grease in with the green beans. Add salt and pepper. Cook, covered, on low heat for however long you like. If you're using fresh beans, cook long enough that all resistance has failed. Drain and serve. Frozen green beans are also uniformly good; I like the frozen green beans with sliced almonds. If you've never confronted frozen veggies that aren't in a cooking pouch, here's what you do: Put the block of frozen food into a saucepan that has a lid. Add about an ounce of water and a pat of margarine. Cover and put on low heat, stirring every few minutes. The block of ice will start to break up as it warms. Don't stir too vigorously or you'll have nothing but little shards of vegetables left. Use a fork and stir gently. No need to drain off the fluid in this instance, as there won't be enough to bother with.

Again, vegetables add color, texture, and a variety of flavors to a meal. They help to make things more interesting than just meat and starch meal after meal. Taken in moderation, vegetables may add some balance to your diet. Leftover veggies are also useful for adding to stew and soup. Most vegetables don't have a lot of germs, so they don't have to be cooked all that long. Many are harmless.

Meat, potatoes, a vegetable, perhaps a salad, some

bread, perhaps a dessert—these have been our basic themes at dinnertime, and, if you've got cooking responsibilities, much of what you do involves numerous variations on this theme. Central to your meal will usually be some part of a dead animal. A pretty disgusting thought, really.

"Our special today is smoked tongue."

"Oh, I couldn't eat anything that had been in an animal's *mouth.* Just let me have some eggs."

Bismarck said that if you were a lover of either laws or sausages, be sure not to be present when either is being made. The late James Beard, when asked if he could possibly eat human flesh, said, "I suppose if there was enough tarragon around. . . ." Survivors of the Uruguayan soccer-team plane crash, stranded for weeks in the Andes, were ultimately forced to eat their departed teammates. They reported that human flesh was pretty bland, and they got to craving salt after a while. The solution: small intestines, dried in the sunshine. They're apparently quite salty. (I'm trying to resist this. I can't. Here I go: I'll bet it took a lot of *guts* to try eating those. There, I feel better now.) Hitler, who evidently considered himself to be a man of high principle, was, according to Albert Speer, a vegetarian.

Okay, no one is going to force you into eating your pet duck. On the other hand, a nice piece of a cow who wasn't a personal friend can be dandy. I'll admit, however, that I once tried mountain oysters (calves' testicles; or, sometimes, those of sheep or pigs), but I couldn't get past the feeling that I was biting into a fallen brother. Once, at a food fair in Omaha, I got Judy to sample "turkey fries" (a part of the anatomy essentially the same as mountain oysters). To my utter shock and surprise, she liked them. This is a woman who would not touch a grit if her life depended on it, nor will she eat cherry pie. (On the other hand, July will voluntarily eat beets. It's hard to figure.) She liked the turkey fries even after I told her what she'd eaten. I was nonplussed until she explained that she thought that eating testicles was a good idea. That shut *me* up for a while.

Meat, for most of us, is where it's at, and beef is the best-seller. Don't come to Nebraska for the fish. I like my roast beef on the rare side; not still kicking, but not cremated, either. If you're of a similar mind-set, then this means that careful attention must be paid to timing, lest a blackened lump emerge from the oven. Buying the best beef you can find is usually worth the trouble and expense. Our system of meat grading actually has to do with fat content: The better marbled the meat is, the more tender and flavorful. There's been some loose talk lately about changing the designations of the lower grades of beef to terms that sound classier. The excuse given for this is the greater interest people have now in leaner (read: tougher) meat. The research certainly hasn't demonstrated, though, that there is any truth to the assumption that leaner beef is going to have any greater food value than an equal portion of beef that is not as lean. I should think that those with health concerns should simply eat *less* red meat altogether. In the meantime, trim off the excess fat on the outside.

I like to get an eye of round roast (sometimes it's called a sirloin roast) that is boneless and has no fat on it at all. It's easy to cook one of these babies until it's dry, so pay attention. How long you cook the thing depends on how *cold* it is. How cold the meat is, not the atmosphere. I try to have both steaks and roasts at room temperature before I cook them. Hamburger, on the other hand, is best dealt with cold. Start roasts at room temperature and note that they generally do better on low heat over a longer time, rather than high heat in a hurry.

This means a 325-degree oven in most cases. Now, the thickness of your roast, its temperature when you start, and how accurate the thermostat on your oven is will all influence how long it takes to cook the thing, so experiment a bit; it is permissible to cut into the roast to see how it's doing. I'll go about an hour and fifteen minutes for a three-pound roast that's fairly thick. You can always cook a roast for a little longer, but it's damn hard to *uncook* it once you've gone too far.

Put the meat in a baking dish; I use a metal one because it's easier to clean. Sprinkle it pretty thoroughly with celery salt and a little less thoroughly with garlic powder. You can use some black pepper, too, if you're of a mind to. Brown it for about twenty minutes in the hot oven, then cover it with a piece of foil to keep the juice in for the remainder of the trip. A really big, bully roast is going to take a lot longer than a little one, of course. After a while, timing these things gets instinctive; I know it's difficult at first and a bit intimidating as well; just keep slicing into the thing to see how it's going.

A word on meat tenderizer. Adolph's 100% Natural Tenderizer is nothing more nor less than dried, powdered papaya plus a little salt. It works, but should be unnecessary unless you're cooking moose or bear. Cooking tough meat a good long time will be more effective at tenderizing it than anything else. Also, remember what we said earlier about slicing it *thin.* Really good meat can seem to be pretty tough if it's served in great rough slabs. Better to do lots of delicate, thin slices.

Meat tenderizer, however, does have its place. Its place in our kitchen for some reason is in the window (well, at least we can always find it). Chemically its effect is to dissolve protein. Foreign protein is what your body reacts to when you've been bitten by a mosquito. She slips a little bit in when inserting her proboscis to suck your blood. It helps to tenderize your hide. Even less appealing is a fly bite; the fly pops a bit of saliva onto you that dissolves your skin so the fly can then drink it. It's foreign protein, as is the venom from a bee sting or wasp sting. In all events, your body seeks to mobilize defenses: isolate, encapsulate, and destroy the invading protein. The afflicted area gets warm, it swells, and it itches. *Folk remedy:* Meat tenderizer can take the itch right out of an insect bite if you can get to it soon enough (like, within fifteen minutes; should you have been bitten an hour or two ago, just forget it and suffer—the stuff has spread out by then). Make a paste of meat tenderizer and a little water on top of the bite, leave it there for about thirty seconds, and then *wash it off* with cool water. The meat tenderizer destroys protein, including the protein in the insect bite. Don't leave it on too long, however, or it will tenderize *you.* I know of a school nurse who put a Band-Aid over a mound of wet meat tenderizer and it ate a hole in the kid. We don't want that to happen to you, so be sure to wash it off. It *does* work. If you misuse the stuff, though, don't come whining to me. Incidentally, if your kid has had an allergic reaction to one bee sting, the next one will be worse. You can get a prescription for a bee sting kit from your doctor. Don't be farting around with meat tenderizer if you're into something serious and need medical help. I've had two friends die from bee stings, so I'm just a bit jumpy about them.

Ponder these thoughts as you mash your potatoes. Having successfully roasted beeves, we are now going to make gravy. This same procedure works, by the way, for other kinds of meat, such as turkey or lamb. The great enemies of good gravy are grease and lumps. If you've cooked a really lean roast, your problem will be not enough juice. With a pot roast or a turkey, though, you will want to get rid of a lot of fat. There are two ways of doing this. One is to tilt the pan, let the grease float to the top, and carefully spoon it off, doing the best you can to just get rid of the grease and not the goody underneath. Or, you can buy a device that looks like a measuring cup that has a spout projecting from the bottom. You pour your juice from the roasting pan into this thing, let it sit for a minute, and pour the good stuff out from under the grease in the cup, which has risen to the top. Neat trick.

If, on the other hand, things are pretty dry in your pan because there wasn't any fat on the meat to begin with, do this: Put the pan in the sink and your cutting board on the counter next to it. Now, as you slice your meat, juice will run out of it (unless you've burned the damn thing up, in which case you'd better start giving some thought to canned gravy). After every few slices, scrape the juice from your cutting board into the roasting pan with a metal spatula. You're going to need to work quickly here, as you should be trying to keep mashed potatoes hot, cut the meat and get it served before it gets cold, and make gravy all at the same time. It doesn't hurt at this point to ask for a little help, someone to take the rolls and the salads and put them on the table; you can reward her later for her good services. When you've got the meat sliced and the last of the juice scraped back into the baking pan, cover the meat with foil and then put a couple of kitchen towels over it as well; this will keep the heat in the meat while you're fixing gravy. Whether you've had to add juice from the slicing of the meat or get rid of extra grease, you now in either event have a pan that has browned meat shards and juices in it. This, believe it or not, *will* be gravy in but a moment.

Remember cornstarch? It *thickens* stuff as it heats. This should give you some ideas. Now, don't go throwing a spoonful of cornstarch into your pan, even if you're in desperate straits. It will immediately form lumps that defy all efforts at removal. I've tried it, so believe me; it's no fun to go lump hunting in a pan of would-be gravy, trying to squash cornstarch lumps with a hamburger flipper.

No, God gave us blenders for a reason. If you've just

made blended whiskey sours, pour the rest into a glass and then swish a little water about in the blender; don't worry if there's a little whiskey left, it may actually improve your gravy. Now take the water you've thoughtfully saved from cooking the potatoes and put about a cup and a half of it in the blender. Add a heaping tablespoon of cornstarch and about a teaspoon of Kitchen Bouquet (which is sort of a brown syrup for darkening gravies and stews; it can be found in the store near the Worcestershire sauce). Out of Kitchen Bouquet? Substitute two shakes of soy sauce. Hit the switch on the blender, having carefully put the top on it first, and grind away for ten seconds or so. Now pour this stuff into the roasting pan and then put the pan on the stove on fairly low heat and keep stirring until everything is good and hot. It *will* thicken as it heats. Too thin? Cook it longer and let it boil just a bit. Too thick? Stir in a bit more water. This method makes surefire gravy every time. It tastes good, offers comfort to the downhearted, and gives the potatoes some needed personality. Just be *sure* to get rid of the grease first.

I find, when stirring gravy, that it helps to use a hamburger flipper; that way you can sort of scrape the bottom of the roasting pan as you stir, which puts the meat drippings into suspension. The gravy will thicken some after being heated. Should you have some left over after the meal, don't be shocked if it forms a relatively solid mass in the refrigerator, almost a kind of jelly. Used gravy is perfectly good and can be reheated; it will thin out again when hot. Just don't leave it out of the refrigerator for four or five hours and then plan to use it again. Remember the principle of How to Not Poison Your Family: Keep food at temperatures of either above 140 or below 40 degrees. This applies to all foods, but I try to be especially careful with meats and gravies, breaded things and stuffings, and creamy things, such as tuna fish or pies.

Keep them either hot or cold and don't let them sit around too long in between.

The beef we get in Nebraska is so good that a common topic of conversation here is the lousy beef someone got while on a trip: "Let me tell you about the crap they call prime rib in Las Vegas." "Oh yeah? It can't be any worse than what I got in Honolulu." Nebraskans will concede that the beef in Iowa is good, too. I was astonished to observe, however, that the legs of lamb in our stores here are frozen and come from New Zealand. I have had wonderful lamb in Wyoming (and in Iceland, too, but that's a bit far to go for a good lamb chop), and it's a mystery to me why we don't get good, fresh lamb in Omaha. We certainly get all the fresh buffalo we want, which isn't much.

It's interesting to note how the country is divided up. The ten years we lived in North Carolina and Georgia we were aware of the north-south division and how it was impossible to get good barbecue outside of a certain geographic district. Now that we live more or less in the center of the country, we're more aware of an east-west dichotomy. I read in the *Wall Street Journal* that Nebraskans who live in New York gather annually for a feast of runzas (sort of a pita pocket bread filled with cooked beef, cabbage, and onions—they're pretty good), Dorothy Lynch salad dressing (made in Columbus, Nebraska), kolachies, and other Nebraska delicacies all flown in specially for the grand feed.

When I'm in New York, I get some sure-enough cheesecake. In San Francisco, it's fresh salmon. Calvin Trillin did three entire books on regional specialties. Most of his material was entirely correct and exceedingly useful (Arthur Bryant's barbecue in Kansas City, however, sucks).

Omaha is still part of the Middle West, especially in terms of food and custom. Going west, the dividing line seems to be where the time zone changes from Central to Rocky Mountain, a little beyond North Platte, Nebraska. Past there, people can unself-consciously wear cowboy boots and hats, something that would turn heads in Omaha. The Denver Airport is a place of confusion and misfortune, because two different kinds of *walkers* are thrown together there.

I've never had a bit of trouble walking (or driving) in New York. This, I think, is because of my Chicago upbringing. Despite the inevitable protest of advocates of either place, I would maintain that New Yorkers and Chicagoans walk the same way: purposefully, usually in a straight line, and trying to avoid eye contact. One can pretty well determine where the other guy is headed and can also count on people preserving a fairly well defined envelope of personal space.

We were just out to southern California, and I was surprised at how often I *stepped* on people. The damn fools would jump right in front of me, weaving back and forth, looking here and there, oblivious of the threat of collisions. At times it was a temptation to pick people up and set them to one side. Coming back, I noticed that eastern walkers in Stapleton International were thrown together with western walkers. There are people marching all over one another in the Denver Airport. Perhaps they're confused by the almost constant public address announcements there: More people are *paged* in the Denver Airport than anywhere else on earth. This confusion and carnage doesn't happen in busy places like Atlanta or La Guardia, or even in Washington National, where everyone is in a hurry in a vain effort to prove that they have important things to do. O'Hare, where more people move about than even in the streets of Calcutta, seldom sees a traffic problem, at least not on the ground. Why, then, the bedlam at Stapleton? Wandering Californians. They're fooled into thinking that they're in a place that's kind of like Los Angeles—which it is—and they let down their guard and get trampled by three CPAs from Philadelphia.

On the other hand, Denver has really great Mexican food. Much better than, say, El Paso, where good Mexican food is seemingly unavailable. Just be careful where you walk. Leg of lamb can be found there as well, and they have good beef. Because of the altitude, however, people in Denver are for the most part unsure of how to cook a pork roast.

Pork roast or leg of lamb work about the same way as roast beef, only you'll want to cook them so that they're brown throughout. Gravy is done the same way as well for these types of meats. I like to get a pork tenderloin that has no fat on it at all, brown it briefly, and then cover it with foil as it bakes. Another good thing to do with one of these is to bake it after covering it with a nice, thick barbecue sauce such as Hunt's Extra Thick and Zesty. Don't cover it as it bakes. I try to buy a tenderloin that's about as thick as your wrist and maybe nine or ten inches long—about a pound and a half. I'll bake one of these at 350 degrees for about an hour, then slice it lengthwise, thin, so that the slices are about nine by three inches or so. Then serve with a little more barbecue sauce dribbled over the top of the slices; no gravy, obviously, with this dish, but pork gravy is usually nothing to write home about, anyway. Also, don't bother trying to make gravy with ham.

A nice way to bake a ham, by the way, is to get a good-size one—either canned or one of the low-fat hams that's boneless—score it with a sharp knife, cutting parallel lines a half inch apart and about a quarter inch deep in a crosshatched diagonal pattern, shove a clove into each of the little squares that you've made with your cross-hatching, place two or three pineapple rings on top, and then pour some maple syrup over the whole thing. Bake at 350 degrees for an hour or longer. Love it.

Ribs can be done in the oven, although they're better,

of course, when done outside on the grill over low heat. However, if you live in an absurd climate like I do and can only look out at your grill under the drifts for several months each year, try this: Take a nice mess of ribs, about three pounds or so, place them in a nine-by-thirteen-inch baking pan, cover them with barbecue sauce, seal the pan over tightly with foil, and bake for at least four hours in a 250-degree oven (preferably longer; I sometimes start these as I go off to work; the house smells *great* when I get home). About an hour before you plan to eat, take the foil off and throw it away (don't be shocked if it has little black holes in it), drain off the grease, which will be considerable, pour more sauce over the top, and put the ribs back in the oven, turning it up to about 325 degrees. These ribs won't win contests, but they're first-rate. Also, much of the fat will have melted off them. The trick is to use low heat over a long time; they'll be nice and tender, too.

Pot roast is best, of course, in a pot, but it can be done in a baking pan as well. I've searched the garage sales until I got a big, old black iron skillet that's about twelve inches across and four inches deep. Get a piece of bone-in pot roast or chuck that's about two inches thick. Now, follow the preparation sequence with care; this is important: Place the meat on a large cutting board, take a big butcher knife, and just whack the hell out of that roast. I mean beat the tar out of it. Pound out parallel lines with the knife, then turn it and pound another direction so the meat looks like it's been gone over with a cat-o'-nine-tails. Turn it over and do it on the other side. This is great therapy and will help you work out any built-up aggression. In the meantime, put the big skillet, if you have one—or a deep frying pan if you don't—on the stove, pour in a quarter-cup of vegetable oil, and turn it on high heat. After scoring the roast, sprinkle it liberally with celery salt, garlic powder, black pepper (coarse grind), and some *flour.* Rub this into the meat. Repeat on the other side. Place several onion slices into the hot oil and start them cooking. Now gently place the pot roast into the pan. Brown it on both sides for about three minutes.

If you don't have a black iron skillet, take the pot roast out of your frying pan at this point and transfer it to a baking pan, then put the onions on top of it. You needn't transfer anything if you're using an iron skillet. In either case, cover the meat now with foil and place in a 325-degree oven; bake for about two and a half hours. About forty-five minutes to an hour before you plan to serve it, take it back out of the oven and add potatoes that have been peeled and quartered, plus several celery stalks and carrots. Add a bit of water at this point if things are looking dry (most often this will not be necessary if you've gotten a nice tight seal with your foil). You can serve everything on the same platter, and you've got nice fixings for gravy, if you want it. Get rid of most of the grease; don't be shocked if this is a considerable amount of fluid. There will still be plenty to work with left in the bottom of the pot or roasting pan. Do your gravy the same way we did a few pages back: water, cornstarch, and Kitchen Bouquet blended and stirred in with the remaining residue in the meat pan. These iron skillets hold the heat, so figure that the handle is one *hot* bugger, even if it's been out of the oven for five minutes; use a pot holder. A minute amount of the iron is scraped into the gravy each time you do this dish, so take comfort and satisfaction in the knowledge that you're giving your family a healthful dose of minerals and helping to prevent anemia.

Something else you can cook up in your big iron pot that will stick to their ribs is beef stew (substitute lamb for beef in this recipe if you're a rich person): Start with a fairly small piece of round steak. You can also go the easy route and purchase what's laughingly called stew beef at the butcher counter; do this if you have especially sharp teeth and massive jaw muscles, as an occasional hunk of bull buffalo seems to sneak into the stew beef every now and again. Cut the round steak into fairly generous bite-size cubes. Chop up a medium-size onion. Now fry three strips of bacon in your iron skillet (an electric skillet will work just fine for this dish; on the other hand, if you really *like* doing extra dishes, fry the bacon in a frying pan and then transfer into a three-quart saucepan). As the bacon is frying, toss in the onion and fry it in the bacon grease. Now toss in the beef cubes and brown them along with the bacon and the onions. After all the meat is nicely browned, turn the heat way down and add about a cup and a half of water, a teaspoon of salt, a half teaspoon of black pepper and a half teaspoon of allspice. Cover it up and simmer on low heat for about an hour. Then, cut up about three peeled potatoes, a stalk or two of celery, two or three carrots, and any other veggies you want. This is a good hiding place, for example, for used peas or green beans. In they go; add some water if things are looking too thick, and then float two bay leaves on the top. After about forty-five minutes, check and see how it's doing. Too watery? Make up a half cup of water and cornstarch in the blender and add it. Too salty? Add another potato. Not salty enough? Leave it alone; the victims can add more salt if they want. Stir this stuff every now and again, being careful not to break up the potatoes as you do it. Just before you serve it, fish out the bay leaves and throw them away.

Omnium-gatherum stew works on this same basic premise. Substitute old pot roast, ham, chicken shards, leftover Polish sausage; you can add anything you want except bananas or Bartlett pears. If you've been a little too free-handed in adding ingredients and get a nasty oil slick on top of your stew, try this: Plop a piece of bread down flat on the top, then immediately fish it out. It will soak up the grease like a blotter. Repeat if necessary. Feed the soggy bread to the dog and you'll have a lifelong friend.

You already know how to cook steak on the grill; here's how to do it indoors on a frying pan. Trim the fat off the edges of your steaks and take a piece of the fat and rub it around the surface of a hot frying pan. Pop the steak onto the greased pan and fry over high heat, making liberal use of the exhaust fan. If you're cooking a steak that's an inch or more thick, put a lid on it and turn the heat down a bit. Have everything else you plan to serve ready to throw on the table; this won't take long. After it's nice and dark on one side, turn it over and repeat. For a fairly thin steak (one-half inch), that's all you do. For a thicker one, slice into it with a steak knife and see if it's done to your liking. Obviously, you can keep on flipping and frying if you want it darker. Easy? No sweat.

A somewhat less grand entrée that's equally easy can be made in a frying pan: cook up however many hamburgers the savages will usually eat, carefully press down on them with the spatula to get as much of the juice out of them as you can, drain it off, and then dump in a can of mushroom soup. Don't add any water; just the concentrated mushroom soup. Stir it around to get it hot. Serve with mashed potatoes or with noodles. The soup has magically turned into gravy.

Heinz, by the way, sells gravy in a jar that's not bad. Don't be afraid to do your own gravy, using a gentle touch and not letting it boil, as it's really quite simple once you get the hang of it. Just remember that you can't really do a whole lot of harm by trying different things. You'll get the hang of it with a little practice. It's good to know, however, about the canned stuff, just to have a backup.

A dish where you definitely won't want to make your own gravy is meat loaf, as almost all the juice left over in the baking pan will be melted hamburger fat. This stuff is no good at all as a base for any kind of gravy, and it should be disposed of. Presumably you keep a can for grease disposal in a handy spot next to your stove. This is, I know unaesthetic. However, I really don't know how you can get around it. Do *not* just go dumping your excess grease into the sink; this is a surefire way to clog your pipes. (If you *should* get grease down your sink, by the way, flush it down with massive doses of very hot water. Drāno is a good product if you must use it, but for God's sake don't keep any leftover around the house. Use it up and dispose of the container.) Getting *rid* of the grease can when you're done with it can be a problem, and it will sure as hell soak the bottom out of your garbage sack if it's tipped. Try this: Use an empty coffee can for excess grease so that you can seal up the top with the plastic lid. The night before your garbage is collected, put the full can in the refrigerator so that it solidifies. Just don't forget to take it out with the rest of the trash. As an alternative, you could mail this to your brother-in-law.

Meat loaf. The foundation of a strong Middle America, the cornerstone of our way of life. Okay, it's hard to get rhapsodic about meat loaf. Meat loaf is like pissing in your pants when you're wearing navy blue: It gives you a warm feeling, but nobody notices it too much. My kids don't much like meat loaf, and I imagine yours don't either. Too bad for them; we always have two menu choices around our house: You either eat it or you don't. No kid who had food set in front of him ever starved to death. Reminding kids that there are people starving in Mozambique, as you probably already know, will not get them to eat their peas or their meat loaf. Generations of parents, however, still try this strategy. Serve your meat loaf with heaping helpings of guilt. It's tradition.

I will admit, right here in front of God and everybody, that meat loaf is old-fashioned. Eating meat loaf is not a yuppie thing to do. My Aunt Lorene made one hell of a good meat loaf, and just about everything about Lorene was old-fashioned. Maybe I'm getting that way, too. I was taken aback a few years ago when I realized that I am now older than most people. I'd always been younger. Many of my students labor under the misapprehension that *new* equates with *good.* I'll cite a source from 1979 and they'll grumble that the data are now too old to be of much use. This is a kind of mental shorthand they use because it's easier than thinking. Rather than read the report and evaluate its worth, one can just dismiss things that are of a particular age. We certainly do this with people. Perhaps it's our constant orientation toward the future. There are students in college now who are astounded to learn that this country put a man on the moon—no mean trick—before they were born.

What's wrong with the kids of today? They don't eat enough meat loaf.

Start with the leanest ground beef you can find. Chop up a medium-size onion and toss it into a mixing bowl. Add the beef, about a pound or a pound and a half. Now, add three-quarters of a cup of Kellogg's Corn Flake Crumbs. Honest. Boxed cornflake crumbs are available; they can be found in the section of the store where you find baking goods. As an alternative, you can make your own, which involves smashing up a bunch of cornflakes with a rolling pin. Bread crumbs are also acceptable. Crack one egg over this mess. Then, add about a half teaspoon of garlic powder and a half teaspoon of celery salt. Now pour about a half cup of catsup in, and, using a clean hand, dig in and mix this stuff all together. Yes, I know it's icky. Steel yourself, rise to the cause, plunge right in, and think of England. When it's all mixed nicely, shape it into a loaf and lay it out in a baking dish. Lay one strip of bacon over the top, then squirt a line of catsup down the middle. Bake at 350 degrees for forty-five minutes or a little longer, depending on how well done you like it. Use two large spatulas to lift the baked meat loaf out of the pan. Use a delicate touch with this, as it's easy to break the thing in half. This goes nicely with Rice-A-Roni or Stove Top stuffing.

Chicken and turkey are, along with catfish, at the top of the list for protein-producing efficiency. Because of this they're fairly cheap relative to other meats. And, they're relatively low in fat. Chickens are also so goddamn stupid that one doesn't mind eating them. As a boy, I was fascinated with various older relatives' systems for the execution of chickens. My dad had big strong hands and wrists and could grasp the chicken by the head, whip the body out away from him, snap back on the head, and pop it off. He could then enjoy the sight of a headless chicken cutting capers about the barnyard. My maternal grandmother would grasp the chicken by the feet and step on its head, turning the body about until the head was twisted off. Grandma was one tough cookie, and you didn't cross her unless you were itching for a fight. Aunts Elsie and Mabel had a sort of guillotine worked out that involved sticking the chicken's head through a hole in the fence. No one, to the best of my knowledge, inquired as to how the chickens felt about all of this. No doubt they had concerns that went unexpressed.

Now that we don't have to kill our own food, I'm content to let the good old days rest. Nostalgia isn't what it used to be. I'd just as soon buy skinless chicken breasts (yes, I know, it's more costly that way) and not have to cope with the neck and giblets, for which I have little use. If I can get skinless and *boneless* breasts, I'm happier still.

Chicken Helper, first cousin to Hamburger Helper, is, to my great shock and surprise, pretty good. Start with a nine-by-thirteen-inch baking dish, toss in the two packets of stuff along with three cups of water, lay out your chicken pieces on top, and bake as directed for forty-five minutes. With this is an envelope of "glaze," which is wretched stuff. Throw it away. Instead, at the forty-five-minute mark, take out the pan, make sure that the stuff under your chicken is stirred up and uniform in terms of moisture, turn over the chicken pieces, and drool over them some sweet and sour sauce, which is available in the section of the store that has Chinese food. Bake for another ten or fifteen minutes. Not bad.

The classic way of cooking chicken, of course, is to fry it. And, a whole frying chicken is about the most economical way of buying meat. One can also buy fryer parts, should you have an aversion to butchering the thing yourself. However, whole fryers can still be found on sale for fifty-nine cents per pound, which is plenty cheap, even if you give the neck and giblets the old heave-ho. Perhaps your cat would enjoy them.

Cutting up a chicken properly takes practice. We were served a dish in Shanghai that we called "fan duck." They evidently take a really large electric fan, about the size of a small Cessna, and toss in the duck while it's on high speed; then they gather up the resultant hunks and cook them. In Beijing, on the other hand, Peking duck (yes, they still call it that) is served split down the middle, so that the two pieces of the head are lying there, nose to nose, looking at each other. I put some seaweed over mine, as I found his reproachful visage to be unsettling. One of the guys in our group, a psychiatrist from Wichita, *ate* the head, which he reported to be very crunchy, particularly the sinuses. Soup is served at the end of a Chinese meal, and we thought that the noodles in this case were particularly tough, until we realized that they were the webbed feet. I've not eaten duck since, nor do I intend to. However, we were about to report how to cut up a whole chicken.

Start with a really sharp knife and the devout hope that you'll be carving up the chicken, not yourself. Be careful; these little suckers are slippery. First, pull each leg away from the body and cut at the joint. It may be necessary to turn the chicken so that each leg is flat on the board as you work on it, for you'll have to put some pressure down to cut through the tough tendons. Now cut away the skin that attaches each thigh to the body, pulling the leg away and cutting it off. Do the same with the wings, being sure to get the upper arms away from the body and cutting at the joint. Now, in theory, you'll have a headless, legless, and wingless bird, which is pathetic, if you stop to think of it. Don't. Cut down either side of the back; there are some thin tips of rib bones along through here that you can mow right through. Ideally you'll thus have the back in one piece, which is not of much use but deserves to be cooked for old time's sake, and a really big piece, the whole breast, left. Split the breast like this: Put it on the board skin side down, place your knife against the breastbone vertically (lengthwise, from the top to the bottom of the bird), and, with the heel of your hand, pop down hard on the back of the knife. This should crack the breastbone and allow you to cut through the breast meat easily. This should leave you with nine pieces of chicken: two breast halves, two wings, two legs, two thighs, and the back. Wash each piece in cold water and lay the pieces out on paper towels. Remember to wash your knife and cutting board (and your hands) thoroughly after dealing with raw chicken; and be particularly persnickety about not cutting anything else with that knife or on that cutting board until after they've been washed. I use liquid Clorox bleach (on the board, not on my hands).

Depending on whether or not you're into chicken fat, you can skin the pieces as you cut up the bird.

Now put a roasting pan, empty, into the oven and turn the heat up to about 375 degrees. Put about a half inch of vegetable oil (I much prefer the bottled liquid kind to the solid, canned variety) into a frying pan and get it good and hot on the stove top. Take two eggs, crack them into a bowl, and beat them up with a fork. In another bowl, pour about a half inch of cornflake crumbs, a bit of salt, and some coarse black pepper, and mix them together with a fork. Substitute flour for the cornflake crumbs if you must; they are, however, a marvel of crunchiness. Now, starting with the larger pieces first, take each piece of chicken, dip it into the egg, roll it around so that it's covered, and shake off the excess. Immediately roll the wet piece of chicken in the cornflake crumbs and then place it, gently, into the hot frying pan. You don't want to splash this stuff. It is our considered recommendation that you wear pants while frying chicken.

Note that you'll not be able to fit all nine pieces into the frying pan at the same time; don't worry about this. Do four big pieces first, then the five smaller ones. Turn each piece over after browning it for about three minutes. After browning on both sides, carefully pick up each piece with tongs and transfer it to the hot baking pan in the oven. If you get your wrist action down right, this can be done without any drips. Once you've got all of it into the oven, obviously you can turn off the burner on the top of the stove and, when it has cooled down some, dispose of the oil in the frying pan. There is nothing, by the way, quite so useful as a big pot cover in the event of a grease fire.

Bake the partially fried chicken for about twenty to twenty-five minutes. Chow down.

This same system can be used for cooking pork cutlets, if you wish, as well as some types of fish fillets.

Broiling, however, is the best way of preparing fish. It works particularly well with big fish, such as salmon, that you can cook in steaks—cross-sectional cuts of the whole fish. This can be done on an outdoor grill (use a piece of foil across the grillwork) or under the broiler of your oven. Start with salmon steaks that are from three-quarters of an inch to an inch thick. One per diner should be adequate, unless you purchased the tail end of the fish. Place one pat of margarine per piece on a cookie sheet and lay each salmon steak down with reverence upon its respective pat. Put another pat of margarine on top of each and then sprinkle a little lime juice on top. Give it a liberal shaking of Lemon Pepper, which can be found in the grocery store's spice section. Broil for four or five minutes, or until the salmon has turned from red to pale pink and has started to get a little crusty around the edges. Take out the cookie sheet and turn the fish over, then pop it back in for another four or five minutes. One wants to get one's timing down to the nth degree here and serve while they're still sizzling. Have folks start on their salads while you're just beginning to cook the fish and serve a side dish, such as au gratin potatoes, that holds its heat so that you're not having to mess with other things while cooking the fish.

My Uncle Al taught me this method for cooking fish, which is in itself amazing, as Al doesn't know jackshit about cooking. He tends to overcook his salmon, but let's not quibble. This is a great way of giving fish a touch of that grilled-outdoors flavor that is much to be desired. Al is also one hell of a fisherman.

Unfortunately most guys who are into fishing usually are, unlike Al, the ones who are least prepared to actually cook the fish. Come to think of it, I know *lots* of fishermen who aren't much good for anything else at all. Seemingly, they've had a problem with the delicate dance we call civilization, a difficulty in taming the brute within, so to speak.

I'm thinking now of my friend Arnold, who's more comfortable off in the woods than he is with people. He's also the kind of selfish son of a bitch who'll buy himself an eleven-hundred-dollar shotgun. I once asked him, "Arnold, what does your wife say when you spend two grand on a fishing trip?" Sensitive and caring individual that he is, Arnold replied, "Ah, she don't mind." Now, it seems to me that Arnold has bought into the great role of the outdoorsman so popular in our culture and so fervently perpetuated by the media. It is the stuff of myths: That is, bullshit. I don't think that the vision of the lone hunter, the island unto himself, works anymore in a complex society. This applies, of course, more to human interaction than it does to hunting and fishing per se.

In a general barroom discussion of breast-feeding, of all things, the proponents (it's better for the kid, not to mention being a money saver) had routed the cons (can't be away from the kid for extended periods, leakage), until Arnold piped up, "I wouldn't let my wife nurse. It would have ruined her figure." I was left gaping. What do you mean, *let* her? Who the hell is Arnold to determine something like that? Then I realized that he was just buying into a particular role.

My friend Jack Balswick wrote a book about this phenomenon: the inarticulate male as cowboy. Don't want a lot of talk; shoot first and ask questions later. Balswick says that the man who can't (or won't) talk about things is simply playing John Wayne (or Gary Cooper, or Clint Eastwood; you make the choice). This is a vastly popular theme in our mythology: the strong, silent type who doesn't say much, but when he rides into town, he really kicks ass. The Seven Samurai. The Dirty Dozen. Confronting evil with an equal or greater evil gives us that vicarious thrill of revenge. Watch Charles Bronson shoot up those drug dealers. See David chop off that Philistine giant's head. Is it any wonder that Ronald Reagan once said that *Rambo* was one of his favorite films? Give us simple solutions to complex problems. Can't win the war? Can't even understand the war? Send in our champion. Screw negotiations; let our gladiator fight for us. Walk softly but carry a big stick; Teddy Roosevelt, our cowboy president.

I'm here to tell you that Conan the Barbarian was a lousy cook.

At least that film was more up front than some of our Westerns. They had old Conan toughing it out with the longest line of dialogue in the movie, a quotation direct from Nietzsche. The king of the Huns asks the boys what is the good life? Conan puts his oar in: "To crush your enemies, see them driven before you, and to hear the lamentations of their women." A tough-guy manifesto. Thus spake Zarathustra. No wonder the Nazis were into Nietzsche.

Balswick says, by the way, that there's another kind of inarticulate male: the playboy. This is the exploiter who loves 'em and then moves on, the role played by Michael Caine in *Alfie.* The pimp instead of the hunter. Balswick, unfortunately, doesn't put himself out on a limb and estimate percentages. I do know that neither type gives great value to the *articulate* male. Oddly, not many women do, either. You'll see a lot more women in the audience watching *Rambo* than you would a movie about, say, Henry Kissinger. Jimmy Carter sweating over getting the Egyptians to sign a peace treaty with the Israelis just doesn't capture the popular imagination. We pay lawyers a lot more than we pay cowboys, perhaps because the work is so much harder. Lawyers are, however, unloved.

It was no great surprise to me when Arnold came into the saloon one day and announced that he would soon be getting divorced. He couldn't understand why she'd moved out on him. For that matter, there were a lot of things that Arnold couldn't understand.

We seem to have shifted the concept of culpability in recent years from interpersonal relationships to physical ills. (Are you sick? It must be your own damn fault! Have you been smoking? Have you been sniffing glue? If you've got AIDS, it's because you're being punished for your sins.) We now have no-fault auto insurance and no-fault divorce. Arnold liked the idea of no-fault; it relieved him of responsibility for his own actions. So what if he'd bought a twelve-thousand-dollar fishing boat?

Arnold, by the way, never did learn to cook (would

John Wayne?), so he's been hungry as well as miserable ever since his handservant took a hike. Arnold, this one's for you, you poor jerk: Grill your fish on aluminum foil with margarine and Lemon Pepper.

How I do run on. Not all fishermen are dipshits, of course. I just wonder how many there are up in the North Woods, afraid to come out because they might have to talk to somebody.

Anyway, this is the way my Uncle Al taught me to cook fish. Being inarticulate has never been *Al's* problem. Sometimes we can hardly shut him up.

This method works well with any big fish; just be careful not to overcook. The rule of thumb with fish is, When in doubt, undercook.

Generally, people in Nebraska view fish with suspicion. I was having some wonderful oysters and seafood gumbo in New Orleans once when some Nebraskans happened along and gaped with amazement as I actually *ate* that stuff. They then ordered hamburgers. Their motto is, "If it doesn't moo, we don't want it."

▸ SOME THOUGHTS ON HOSPITALITY

I like to feed people something they wouldn't ordinarily be eating elsewhere and—I hope—give them a meal they'll remember. Memories of good fellowship and jolly times about the dinner table are what it's all about. Figure that the odds are that fewer than one hundred people will show up for your funeral. What will they remember you for? I think we have a certain obligation to our guests. Don't let them remember you for your cheapness.

Why do they always refer to an abundant table as a

"groaning board?" Because there's so much heavy food there that it weights down the boards of the table and makes them groan? Close, but no cigar. It's because the *diners* are weighted down so much that they leave the table groaning.

Now, if you're into bean sprouts and tofu and little pissant stuff like that, go ahead and skip this next section. If, however, you enjoy a memorable meal every now and again made up of sure-enough food ("If I'd wanted fiber, I'd have eaten the doormat"), then read on. You know you've been a good host and pleased your guests when they come up to you after the meal with tears in their eyes, kneel, and kiss the back of your hand in gratitude. Just be prepared for this and also be prepared to help them back up. By the way, it seems appropriate to tell you at this point that the original meaning of the word "vomitorium" was a large, archlike exit in a Roman amphitheater that would allow many people to leave at one time. That just came to mind, so I thought we'd deal with it.

One would think that if you fed them really well one time, they'd stay fed. This is the philosophy I used with friends once when I gave them shrimp cocktail, lasagne, and filet mignon. One woman actually took home a doggie bag. Now, the lasagne is a meal in itself, and we'll get to that shortly; let's just briefly review the other things: filet mignon is just a thick steak; cook it on a frying pan at high heat with the exhaust fan on. I use a griddle with a nonstick surface, but I also put a slight amount of vegetable oil on it; I'm taking no chances of sticking when it comes to prime filet that goes for eight dollars a pound. Put a lid on the pan as the filets cook, and cook by *sight* rather than by time—you can see when they're about done. With really thick filets, you may have to cook them for a while on their sides as well as on their tops and bottoms. Probe every now and again to see how it's going;

it would be a shame to overcook fine steak. The shrimp cocktail is just as easy and can be prepared an hour or more ahead of time, as you'll be wanting to serve it cold. Obtain fresh, unpeeled shrimp that are of moderate to large size (yes, I know that *large shrimp* is an oxymoron). Shrimp are sold by number per pound; twenty-four to thirty per pound are pretty good size. I'd plan on five of these per happy eater.

Keep your shrimp cold until ready to deal with them. Boil a big kettle or Dutch oven full of water, add a teaspoon of salt, and toss in all the shrimp at once when the water boils. They'll turn from gray-brown to pink immediately. Boil for three minutes, no more. Immediately dump into a colander and rinse with cold water. Then put all the shrimp into a bowl of cold water that has some ice cubes in it. You want to cool these babies down fast, as the last thing you want is an overcooked, mushy shrimp. Peel them quickly and then put the peeled shrimp back into the refrigerator. About fifteen or twenty minutes before it's time to eat, put some shredded lettuce and chopped celery into old-fashioned glasses, one for each person, about half full. Arrange the shrimp around the edges of the glasses and put them out on the table along with a bottle (or a bowl, if you're being fancy) of seafood sauce—the red kind (Heinz makes a good one) that you'll find right by the catsup in the store. No other salad is needed, as this had better be good enough for them.

The lasagne is the most complex dish found in this book, but it's not only worth the investment of time and energy, it's also astonishingly easy to prepare. It will also make your reputation. I swear it. You will be honored among your peers; this will also spoil you for all other lasagnes. I have *never* tasted restaurant lasagne that is as good as mine, and I am a student of fine lasagnes. Assembly of this stuff will take you about half an hour, and figure on baking it for another forty-five minutes. You'll also want to let it rest for five minutes before cutting into it.

Now pay attention; everything else has been foreplay. This is the thing itself.

You're going to need one of the small packages of lasagne noodles (they contain ten noodles, which is one extra). You'll also need a small can of mushroom pieces, a medium-size onion, a pound or so of either Italian sausage or hamburger, a six-ounce package of sliced provolone, a sixteen-ounce package of sliced mozzarella, grated Parmesan and grated Romano cheeses (Kraft sells them together as "Italian Blend" in a white and green cylindrical paperboard container), two of the fifteen-ounce cans of Contadina tomato sauce, and the following spices: garlic powder, coarse black pepper, red cayenne pepper, flaked (not powdered) oregano, and sweet basil leaves.

When the Water Rat was trying to whip things into shape at Mole's house, he sent the Hedgehog children to the store for a few things, including marmalade: "And be sure it's Fortnum's, for I'll have no other." I don't know (or care) if Fortnum and Mason's makes tomato sauce; I do, however, know just how Ratty felt. Make sure it's Contadina, for I'll have no other. On the other hand, fresh mushrooms have no particular virtue in this dish; I've tried it both ways, and the canned ones are fine.

Grease the bottom of a nine-by-thirteen-inch baking pan. Fill a Dutch oven with hot water, a teaspoon of salt, put a lid on it, and put it over high heat on the stove. Preheat the oven to 325 degrees. Peel and chop the onion into fairly substantial pieces; little tiny ones would get lost in the shuffle with this dish. Begin to sauté them in a couple of tablespoons of vegetable oil in a large frying pan. As soon as the water starts to boil, turn the heat down to low-medium and add the lasagne noodles. Don't just dump them in; you'll find that you need to *layer* them in order to make them fit; try to keep from breaking them. You'll want to boil the noodles for about ten minutes, then rinse and drain them; leave them in the colander until you're ready for the assembly.

Pour off the juice from the canned mushrooms and rinse them with fresh water, then drain and add them to the frying onions. Now crumble the hamburger over the onion-mushroom mixture. If you've opted for Italian sausage instead of hamburger, you'll need to slice the links lengthwise and remove the skins, then crumble the meat into the frying pan. In either event, cook until the meat browns, breaking it up and stirring every now and again. Now, open up the cheese packages and the cans of tomato sauce.

I know that this all sounds very complex and that you're moving about like a one-armed paper hanger. Trust me; it's not all that bad. Once you get your moves down and have two or three things going at the same time, you'll be like an orchestra conductor. Or maybe more like a streetcar conductor. Whatever. By the way, evict any small dogs or children that you might trip over while all of this is happening. You want room to maneuver while you're assembling this stuff.

Once the cooked meat is brown, drain the grease off. All of it. Your noodles should be about done at this point; stick a knife in one and test for tenderness. Remember to rinse them really well and shake off all the water. Put your baking dish on the counter next to the sink, the pan of cooked meat and onion on the other side of that, and arrange your cheeses, spices, and tomato sauce. You are now ready for the assembly.

Stop at this point and get in touch with your feelings. Reflect on the fact that ricotta cheese is an adulterant that has ruined both the taste and the aesthetics of too many lasagnes throughout the years. We won't let that happen to *our* lasagne, will we? Also, it's my sad duty to inform you that there are people who actually put cottage cheese into lasagne. Dismiss all thoughts of physical punishment; we're above that.

Put the first three noodles side by side lengthwise into the baking dish, and on top of them lay down half the mozzarella (it's okay if the cheese slices overlap; don't let that rattle you). Spoon on about a third of the meat-onion-mushroom mixture and pour over this about two thirds of a can of tomato sauce. Sprinkle liberally with the oregano and basil, less liberally with the black pepper, and sparingly with the cayenne pepper and garlic powder. Shake a goodly amount of the grated cheese onto this.

Now lay down another layer of the noodles. On them place all of the Parmesan cheese. These are round slices, so break up a few pieces to make it fit. Then, another layer of the meat, another two thirds of a can of tomato sauce, and more spices and grated cheese. Smells good, doesn't it? You're doing just fine. We're almost there.

On top of this lay down your last three lasagne noodles, then the rest of the mozzarella; over the cheese sprinkle the last of the meat-onion-mushroom blend. Pour the last of the tomato sauce over this and then give it a liberal shaking with the grated cheese, covering the top not unlike a sudden snowstorm. Now go to it with the red pepper, the black pepper, the basil, and an extra dose of the oregano. What? You've discovered a little residue in one of the tomato sauce cans? Dribble it on artistically. Run your finger around the edge of the baking pan to knock off the excess grated cheese and spices. What the hell, give the top a shot with the garlic powder. Contemplate your creation.

It's best that you bake this right away (forty-five minutes in a 325-degree oven and five minutes' rest after baking prior to cutting); however, it is permissible to make this ahead of time and keep it in the refrigerator as long as a day before serving. It can also be frozen, but, as in cryogenics, this does take the life out of the thing. You'll have enough with this recipe to serve eight, so there will likely be leftovers. This stuff keeps well in the refrigerator, although I'd suggest transferring the leftovers to a clean pan. Otherwise, if you warm the residue over again in the original baking pan, you're twice baking the crust into your baking dish, thus making a double cleaning problem. Refrigeration of the leftovers actually seems to make this lasagne more mellow; the flavors have a chance to sort of swap around and get into each other. At any rate, serve nice and hot; it goes best with garlic bread and tossed salad and makes a magnificent main dish or a truly impressive side dish for steak or fish.

My Aunt Carrie is particularly partial to this lasagne, and I try to make it when she visits; I even made it once when I visited her. Carrie is not only a sweetheart but also a person who taught me a lot about courage. She had a cancerous lump last year and had to have a breast removed. She called me up: "Jim, they cut off one of my boobs." Carrie prefers a direct approach.

"Gee, Carrie, I'm sorry to hear that."

"Yeah, and it was one of my favorites, too."

I've got to admire Carrie's way of coping with crisis. My own preferred method is to run back and forth wailing.

There *is* a correlation between consumption of lasagne and courage. And, like the Powdermilk Biscuit, this stuff will give you the strength to do what needs to be done.

Now, you and I know that there are any number of ego needs that are met by entertaining and cooking something yourself for your guests. I often serve homemade strawberry jam with hot biscuits when we have company. They practically fall out of their chairs when they learn that I made the jam (any idiot can make strawberry jam; just follow the recipe on the bottle of Certo). Because you're a man, not much is expected of you. This is Nature's way of compensating us for having shorter lives. (As a gerontologist, I can't resist throwing this in: There's a way of lengthening average life expectancy among males that actually *is* backed up by years of research, and it goes beyond worrying yourself into an early grave over how much you should jog. The fact is, steers outlive bulls and capons outlive roosters. Are you willing to undergo the unkindest cut of all? I don't want to know about it.)

Anyway, you know that others will be inordinately impressed should you show the least little ability around the kitchen; you needn't be so brash as to brag about your accomplishments—they'll speak for themselves. There's more good news: You don't actually *have* to be a great cook to get credit; just do a few things well. Once you have a reasonable number of things you can cook down pat, all you have to do is vary the combinations and every now and again add something to your repertoire. I'll let you in on a little secret: Your guests don't really expect gourmet cooking; in fact, there's a lot that can go wrong with fancy-pants stuff. Just do a reasonable job with a few good things and the world will sing your praises. It will be so much better than what they *expect* that they'll go wild. And the really important thing is that you're sharing something of yourself by feeding your friends.

When my old pal Merle and I cook the monthly breakfast at church, we have him sample the coffee. If he doesn't go blind, then we know that it's safe for others to drink. We figure that Merle has led a full life. So think of it this way: Have you got a few excess kids? Are some of them uglier or snottier than the others? Try out your first efforts at cooking on them. If they make it, then it's probably all right to feed the stuff to other people.

As you get more and more sure of yourself, you can work up to a real banquet with confidence of your success.

Now, there's nothing intrinsically difficult about a Thanksgiving turkey dinner or any of its component parts. In fact, we've already covered just about everything that goes into such a dinner. Throwing such an event seems like a lot of work and bother because there are many dishes that go into it; but none of the dishes themselves are all that tricky.

Scheduling is the tricky part. Try to get as many things done ahead of time as possible, because there are several that have to be done at the last minute, and remember that the oven is already tied up with bigger things than your biscuits. In fact, plan on serving hard rolls straight out of the sack from the bakery; you'll have enough going on without worrying about bread at the very last.

This implies that you'll give this whole event some planning. Remember two things: Screw up the gravy and they'll think they had a bad meal no matter how hard you try with everything else; and a turkey dinner is just about the cheapest meal you can feed a mob. Keep these verities before you as you endeavor to persevere.

Okay, planning. Here's what you plan: Figure that a green salad will be a pain in the ass to fix at the last minute, and it really doesn't go with Thanksgiving dinner anyway. Scratch that. We've already vetoed hot biscuits. Better plan on a big thing of Jell-O (you can make progressive multiples, just use a larger dish, more water, and more packages of Jell-O; you are allowed to do this—just keep an accurate count on your proportions), and you'd also better plan to throw some fruit in the Jell-O. This is something you can do ahead of time. Also, serve a relish tray with black olives, carrot sticks, some pickles, and celery sticks. Easy enough, and also something you can do hours ahead of the crisis. You'll have to have pie; it's the law. You can make pies the day before. I'll tell you how to do it in the next section. Or, even better, try this one: Someone will inevitably open her big trap and say, "Is there anything I can bring?" So what if she doesn't really mean it? You've got her. Say, innocently, "Why, yes, how about bringing along a couple of pies?" That'll close *her* out.

Cranberries. Don't fall into the trap of making your own. Buy a couple of cans of jellied cranberry sauce. Keep them cold, then open both ends of the can and shove the cylinder out onto a little plate. You've planned on hard rolls from the bakery; put out a couple of plates of butter as well.

Veggies. Nobody will be too interested in veggies, so serve some green beans. All you've got to do is keep them hot on the back burner. Also, sweet potatoes. Forget the raw ones; they're for fanatics. Get two of the big cans of sweet potatoes (they may call them yams on the can; nobody can tell me the actual difference between a sweet potato and a yam; please, don't you be the first). Drain off most of the juice. Warm them up in a large saucepan. Dump them into a serving dish. Decoratively place eight or ten marshmallows on top, sprinkle on a tablespoon or so of brown sugar, and dribble a little maple syrup over the whole mess. Now microwave until the marshmallows melt, probably about two minutes, depending on how hot the yams were to begin with. Serve with chutzpah.

Well, you can throw in whatever little doodads you can think of, but it seems to me that most all of the meal is accounted for with these things that are either done ahead of time or no trouble to do within a few minutes of zero hour. The mashed potatoes, the gravy, and the bird and stuffing are the big deal here. You can peel up enough potatoes an hour before the turkey comes out of the oven and have them simmering in just enough water to cover them; they'll be ready to mash by the time the turkey's done (by the way, save that water the spuds have cooked in; you'll be wanting it for the gravy).

Incidentally, try to enforce a little discipline around your place about getting to the table when the food is served. I'm forever trying to search out the bunch I live with just when everything is hot. It's bad enough that I have to feed them; it's a real insult to have to go *find* them and then feed them. And they wonder why I'm such a crank at dinnertime. Bastards. Judy's favorite trick is to start running a tubful of hot water just when she hears the oven door open. She's happier if she's soggy while she eats.

▸ HOW TO COOK A TURKEY

I remember when I was a little kid and my mother would take me along to the butcher shop on Western Avenue in Chicago, where there was an old Armenian who kept turkeys and chickens in cages. You'd pick out the victim, which would be carted off to the back room, and suddenly you'd hear "Whop!" when the cleaver would fall. The dripping package would then be toted home in my brother's red wagon, and she'd spend the next hour going over the corpus with tweezers, getting rid of the remaining pinfeathers. It's no wonder that I didn't eat much turkey as a kid.

When Fat Freddie bought a live turkey, the butcher asked him if he planned to do anything weird to the bird. He said, "Oh, no. I'm going to kill it and eat it." The execution was very humane; he gave it an overdose of reds. Phineas and Franklin thought the meal was quite good and wondered what Freddie stuffed it with. "I didn't have to stuff it; it wasn't empty."

It seems to me that having the bird arrive frozen hard as a rock in a thick plastic wrapper is much more satisfactory. Buy the kind that has the little pop-up button that will tell you when it's done. Also, figure that a fourteen-pound bird will feed eight people easily with plenty left over for sandwiches tomorrow. And, when you see "more than enough to stuff a fourteen-pound bird" printed on the side of the Pepperidge Farm stuffing package, believe them. You won't need two. Unless you've won the raffle down at the Saint Vitus bazaar, forgo the temptation to bring home a twenty-pounder. It will hang over the edge of your roasting pan and drip slop on the floor of the oven. Leave the thing in the sink the night before you're to cook it; these babies take some little time to thaw. If it's still frozen somewhat when the time comes, it is permissible to run hot water into the thing; the asshole was enlarged at the factory for just this purpose.

Speaking of which, when Judy Daniel baked her first turkey, I got the honors when carving time came, since John had never done one. Judy Daniel is a bright and beautiful person and I love her, but I did detect a fold of paper sticking out of where the stuffing should have been. Right. The neck and giblets, still wrapped up. Inquiries were, of course, made, and Judy explained, "I didn't want to stick my *hand* in there!" Well, let's admit you to the *cognoscenti,* just on the off chance that you don't know quite what I'm talking about. The turkey, as you might know, is sold by the pound. In a blatant attempt to increase the weight of the bird that you buy, the processor has taken the neck and the internal organs, wrapped them in a paper envelope, and shoved them back into the abdominal cavity, not unlike a pathologist completing an autopsy. Thus about a pound of useless stuff is added to the weight of the purchase you make. (Why do they always refer to it as hanging weight? They don't hang these mothers; they chop their heads off.) At any rate, your task, should you choose to accept it, is to reach right up in there and drag this unfortunate package out. Then either throw it out, feed it to the cat, or, if you're really pissed at the bank, put it into a safe-deposit box. It helps to do this while warm water is flowing into the body shell; you're supposed to wash the thing anyway. Shake all of the water out and place the bird on a roasting rack in a large pan. Stuck for a big enough roasting pan? They sell throwaway aluminum foil roasting pans in the supermarket. A roasting rack is a metal device that holds the turkey up off the bottom of the pan, out of the melted grease, so that the hot air can circulate under it.

Now, that package of stuffing you bought has directions printed on the side of it: Basically you mix the bread crumbs together with hot water, melted margarine, and some chopped onion and celery. I like raisins in it as well, which irritates my mother no end. Two things are important here: Have clean hands when you do this; it's safe to assume that you've just handled a turkey that has more than enough bacteria on it; and the bugs multiply in wet bread like crazy, so don't let it sit around. Make the stuff, shove it up the turkey's ass, and pop it in the oven without dillydallying. If there's too much stuffing to fit in the turkey, put the remainder in a baking dish and refrigerate; you can bake it for forty-five minutes tomorrow when you're serving the leftovers.

Our friend Ilene the Martyr sits up all night so that she can baste the turkey every fifteen minutes. Ilene is also a few bricks short of a full load. A word about basting a turkey: Don't. It serves no purpose whatsoever, cools down the oven so that the baking time is lengthened, and keeps you from doing better things. Do this: Just before popping the culprit into the oven, rub it with vegetable oil (*not* butter or margarine, which contain salt and will dry it); this will give it a nice golden color as it bakes. After the first hour, cover the top with a sheet of aluminum foil; this will also help to keep it from drying out. I have not noticed, by the way, that so-called self-basting turkeys are any moister than any other kind.

Figure on about fifteen to twenty minutes per pound in a 350-degree oven, or until the little plastic button pops up. One can also wiggle the leg; if it seems to pull loose from the body and everything else is ready to go, pull that bird out of the oven regardless of what the plastic button says. I've had defective ones that wouldn't pop during a cremation. One other nice thing about the modern turkey, by the way, is the wire device that grows in its crotch, right down there in front of the pope's nose. You use this thing to tuck the legs together modestly right after you've rammed in a quart of wet bread crumbs. I can recall Mom going to it with a darning needle and button thread to seal over the wound. No more of that. I'm not sure how they breed the birds so that they'll have this wire growing there (shades of the *Story of O*), but one can only conclude that genetic engineering is a marvel.

It's a prevalent old wives' tale that one must let a turkey cool down prior to carving it. Horsefeathers. What purpose could that possibly serve? Yes, give it a minute or two for the flash heat to dissipate, but get right to work on the thing as soon as you can handle the heat. This is where things get busy in the kitchen, and it would be nice if you could recruit some help, should you have some trustworthy person who won't trip all over the place.

Right before taking the bird out of the oven, do this: Drain the water off the potatoes into the jar of your blender. Mash the potatoes with a pat or two of butter and a little (two ounces or less) milk, using an electric hand mixer. Cover the mashed potatoes and put them on the back burner on the lowest heat setting you can achieve. Now toss a heaping tablespoonful of cornstarch and a goodly glob of Kitchen Bouquet into the potato water in the blender; hit the high button for ten seconds just to mix it up a bit. Leave it there for the moment.

Take the turkey out of the oven and use this procedure: Put oven mits on each hand and wad up a couple of pieces of paper towel in each; grab the turkey on either side just back of the wings and lift it off the baking rack and onto your carving board. At this point, get your helper busy sucking the grease out of the baking pan. Most of the fluid will be melted fat and should be disposed of; you'll still have plenty of cracklings in the pan to flavor the gravy. Failure to get rid of enough grease will ruin both your gravy and your reputation, so be fastidious about this. (My sister, Elaine, once said, "I'm not fastidious, but I *am* bigtitious." She, by the way, makes excellent gravy.) After the grease is satisfactorily removed, you can pour the mixture from the blender into the baking pan. This ought to give you plenty of gravy; if not, a bit more water blended with cornstarch can be added. Remember, resist the temptation to add cornstarch directly to the cooking gravy. It will lump up right away and defy all attempts at destruction. The gravy will thicken as it cooks, so place the roasting pan on a large front burner over low heat and have your confederate posted there stirring things with a spatula while you carve the bird. Turn the heat down to almost nothing while the gravy thickens.

Carving a turkey is not all that imposing a task, really. I find an electric knife to be helpful, and I also keep my carving board close to the sink so that I can use a scraper to rid it of the excess juices that are inevitable. Also, to try to help keep down the mess, I use ample paper towels and also have a doubled-up set of brown paper bags at my feet. This is where I throw the wings first thing, as nothing is quite so useless as a turkey wing ("Oh! I *like* turkey wings!" Very well, madam, send me the postage and I'll mail you mine).

Pull the ends of the legs out of the wire crotchguard, spread, and scoop the stuffing out into a serving bowl; a long-handled kitchen spoon is obviously the tool of choice for this D & C procedure.

Next cut the legs off. You can either leave them as drumsticks, should someone at your table have a penchant for playing Henry VIII, or else hold them by the narrow end and run your knife down, slicing off the dark meat. Long, thin bone splints will appear; pluck them out and discard them. Now dig in and get the thighs cut away from the body; it may be necessary to grip the bone ends with a wad of paper towels in order to keep from burning your fingers. Slice the dark meat off of each of the thighs and, if you can dig around and find them, of the upper wings as well. I throw the skin and bones away as I finish stripping them; I probably lose a few good ounces of meat in this quest at keeping the mess down.

At this point, get whatever help you have to put the sweet potatoes on the table on a hot pad, scoop the mashed potatoes into a bowl and onto the table, and put the gravy into a boat or serving dish. Get the beans and the bread out; in fact, everything should be on the table along about now; you've got your meat platter half-filled and things are narrowing down to a climax ("Well, where do you want *me* to sit?" I don't give a good goddamn. Just sit down, shut your big yap, and enjoy yourself.)

Split the breast skin lengthwise right down the middle. Slip your knife under that golden skin, pull it away from the meat, and throw it away. That's right. It's not good for anything. I once knew a pervert who *liked* turkey skin. He also liked little girls' shoes.

Still facing the bottom of the bird, take your knife and cut down on either side, slicing off nice big pieces of white breast meat. Cut it down to the bone as well as you can, given the time constraints, and then bring the beautiful pile on out to your now-salivating diners. You can take a paring knife to cut off the little remaining hunks after dinner. Get these wrapped up and into the refrigerator within a reasonable time. Should you have just an enormous amount of leftovers, freeze some of them for a few weeks from now; three days of turkey in a row is enough for anybody.

There, see how easy that was?

My understanding is that, given an unlimited supply of available food, vultures will eat until they can no longer stand and then fall on their sides and continue eating. Judy's Uncle Walter was like that; he'd just unhinge his jaw and tip back the fridge. To me, the goal of a good meal is to feed them really well, not so that they'll fall on their sides but just so that you can keep dessert simple. If you're going to do something elaborate, do it with the meal itself. Don't bust your ass on dessert only to hear half of them say, "Oh, I've cut out *all* desserts; I've *got to cut down*!" Screw that. So feed them good in the first place and let dessert be a no-sweat proposition. Keep it light.

I've never really gotten into trouble for feeding people. I figure that they have good enough sense to eat what they like and however much they like. You don't have to stand over them with a bread knife like Portnoy's mother and force it down their throats. (Of course, I'm not above cajoling a recalcitrant child: "Eat that or your eyes will fall out.") Generally, though, something sweet and simple for the end of the meal is appropriate if you've done your job well up to that point.

Now that I think of it, I *did* get into trouble once for feeding a *bear*. This harpy with an unusually ugly little nose picker in tow accosted me once at the zoo after I'd thrown a couple of peanuts to a Sumatran sun bear. "Sir! Don't you read anything? These animals are on a controlled diet, blah blah, on and on. . . ." I was so astonished that I actually stood there and got lectured by this harridan. One never thinks of the right thing to do. Feed *her* to the bear? We'll see about controlled diets. The bear couldn't believe his ears, either. I imagine he was glad to see her leave. No more desserts for him.

CHAPTER 5

Dessert

Now, on to desserts. Again, because you're a man, little is expected of you in terms of your ability to make desserts. This works rather nicely with our philosophy of keeping it simple, doesn't it? Almost anything will do, or even be greeted with shouts of joy. A simple cup of fruit sherbet is good. Or, try this: Put a scoop of vanilla ice cream on top of a slice of Sara Lee pound cake and drizzle a little crème de menthe over the top.

Or you can simply serve individual bowls of ice cream with chocolate sauce. Go wild and hit each of them with a shot of whipped cream from a spray can. Sure, sprinkle some broken pecan or walnut pieces over the top. Big deal. As an alternative, if you've got ice cream but no chocolate sauce, just serve crème de menthe sundaes: vanilla ice cream with a little booze over the top. Simple and tasty.

Okay, let's say that you're out to impress the divorcée of your dreams. You've already fed her rare roast beef and she knows that you made the gravy personally. You've given her one perfect rose. You've already let on that your car is paid for and that you are a member of a pension plan. What to do next? Feed her pie.

That's right, pie. Her very heart will melt.

Now, not just any old pie will do for an occasion like this. Frozen pie is just fine, but let's not miss the point here: What's wanted is pie made by your own fingers. I know, I'm just a romantic old fool. Here's how you do it:

Pie, as you probably already know, has to have a crust, and there's the rub. Yes, it is possible to buy ready-made piecrusts in those little throwaway tinfoil pans. Doing this, however, violates the rules, and you might as well just get a whole ready-made pie (Mrs. Smith's Natural Juice fruit pies are the frozen pies of choice). But, really, it's those little imperfections, obvious to one and all, that prove that you are indeed the author of the pie you set before the ones you love. Frozen pies don't have any imperfections.

Now, it's actually easier to *show* someone how to make a piecrust than to describe it. Send me a plane ticket, I'll come help. The first thing to remember is this: If you screw it up, you can ball up the dough again and try over; piecrust is very forgiving. Start by washing your hands, especially if you've been reading a newspaper, as smudges *will* show in this stuff and make a bad impression. Next, take out the good old piecrust sticks.

Piecrust sticks. Sounds kind of funny, right? Piecrust sticks are a product made by Betty Crocker and available in the cake mix section of the store. It's legal to use these. While you're at the store, pick up one or more Teflon pie pans. They're well worth the extra cost.

The last thing you want to do is actually make piecrust dough from a recipe. Trust me on this one. The piecrust sticks are simplicity itself. You just break one of them up into a small bowl, dribble two tablespoons of hot water over it, stir it up with a fork until it globs all together, and you've got perfect pie dough. Now comes the tricky part. Getting the pie dough from a sticky ball into a nice, flat bottom crust takes some dexterity, and this will come with practice, but it's a frustrating thing at first. Take comfort in the thought that, after a while, making piecrust is just like riding a bicycle: Once you learn how, you never forget.

Start with a clean section of countertop. Take a medium-size handful of flour, spread it about on the countertop, and also rub some on your rolling pin. Flop the ball of sticky dough right down in the middle of the floured countertop and kind of roll it around by hand so that it picks up flour on the outside of the ball and loses its stickiness. Shove a little more of the loose flour toward the center of your work area. Now start mushing down on the ball with the palm of your hand, flattening it as you go; turn it over in the flour every now and again as you do this. It's getting bigger around as it flattens out, right? Good. Keep doing this, flattening it with your hand until it's become like a really big pancake, about half an inch thick. *Now,* go to it with the floured rolling pin, working around so that the dough stays circular as you flatten it further. Sort of eyeball your pie pan; you'll see when you've gotten the dough flattened out so that it's big enough to fill the pan.

It should be about an eighth of an inch thick at this point, and just picking it up and flopping it into the pan is impossible without tearing it all to hell. Here comes one of the real tricks of the trade, so pay attention. Get out your largest spatula or hamburger flipper, and gently run it underneath the dough to loosen it and keep it from sticking to the countertop. Pull out the spatula. *Then* sprinkle flour over half of your circle of crust; lightly rub it about. Next slip your spatula back under the unfloured half and fold it over onto the floured part. Now put *two* flippers under the folded dough and transfer it over into the pie pan; unfold it in the pan and it should cover. It won't, of course, cover exactly right on your first few tries. Get it to cover as much as you can. Then, take a sharp knife and trim around the sides, cutting off the overhang. Use these trimmings to patch in the vacant and torn spots in your crust. Just mush the pieces together with your fingers; this is the bottom anyway and doesn't have to look good. Once you've gotten it laid out to your satisfaction, go over it with a fork, lightly pricking it here and there. Don't go wild; an inch apart will do. So now you've got the bottom of a pie.

The middle is the easy part. They sell cans of pie filling in the store: cherries, apples, peaches, blueberries. Have you got a big pie pan? Buy a big can of pie filling. Peach pie, by the way, works much better with fresh peaches. Wash and thinly slice six cups of *ripe* peaches. Sprinkle with a teaspoon of lemon juice to keep them from turning brown. Mix in a cup of brown sugar, a quarter cup of flour, and two shakes of cinnamon. You've got peach pie filling. If you really want to go the extra mile, peel the peaches before you slice them.

The top of the pie should be the most difficult, because it's there for all to see and it's thus harder to conceal your screwups. That's why we make *lattice-topped* pies. You're going to crosshatch strips of piecrust over the top and have the thing look fancy. This is actually ever so much easier than getting a good cover without tearing a whole top crust. Simply crumble up another piecrust stick with a couple of tablespoons of hot water, roll the dough out on a floured surface like you did with the bottom crust, and rub a tiny amount of flour across the top. Now, take a sharp knife and cut the whole thing into strips that are about a half inch wide. Gently run your spatula under the strips, loosening them, and pick them up one by one. Lay them down over the pie filling about a half inch apart. Do the vertical layer first, starting with the longer pieces for the middle of the pie, obviously, and working your way to the edges with the proportionately smaller ones. You don't have to interweave them, just lay down half of them in one direction and then the remaining half in the other; this gives the impression of a lattice. Turn the pie and lightly pinch down the ends so that they merge with the dough from the bottom crust. Looking good.

Have your oven preheated to around 425 degrees. If your pie is quite full, some of the filling may boil out of it, so put it on a cookie sheet or pizza pan that has a piece of foil on it. Just before you pop it into the oven, sprinkle about a teaspoon of plain white sugar over the top; this will make it crunchy. Should you be willing to really go the extra mile, use *pearl sugar* on top of the pie instead of the regular granulated type. We had a Swedish foreign exchange student live with us a few years back. She taught me this one. Fia was diligent in searching out the few items in American stores that were fit to eat. One day she came home with a small pink box labeled *pärl socker.* On the back side it said *pearl sugar.* This is white sugar made up into bigger pieces, about the size of rock salt. Sprinkle about a tablespoon of this evenly across the lattice top. Bake for about thirty minutes, or until the top is brown. It's important to put it in an oven that's already hot. If you put it into a cold oven and then turn the heat on, your bottom crust will be soggy. Don't cut a fruit pie while it's still hot, or everything will run all over the place. So, if you're planning on serving pie, give yourself a couple of hours before the meal to bake it and let it cool down. Serve with a scoop of vanilla ice cream on top. Nothing better.

You also can make little individual pies; small foil pie pans are sold in the store in the same section where they have paper cups and such. These, officially, are tarts. Wow.

Pecan pie requires no crust at all on top, so you can hardly go wrong. This stuff is rich enough that you'll want to serve only small pieces. Mix three eggs, three-quarters of a cup of brown sugar, a cup of Karo syrup, a stick of margarine that you've melted, and a teaspoon of vanilla. Add a cup of pecan pieces and pour the whole mess into a newly made pie shell (you can roll it out ahead of time and then keep it in the refrigerator). Bake the little beauty at 375 degrees for forty-five minutes, or until the pecan filling starts to get kind of solid in the middle. Serve with a shot of whipped cream.

Pumpkin pie doesn't require any lid on it either. I'm not at all wild about plain pumpkin pie, but, made with a little booze in it, the stuff's not bad at all: Make your pie bottom, beat together a can of pumpkin, a can of Pet evaporated milk, and a cup of brown sugar. Then beat in three eggs, a quarter cup of bourbon or brandy, a teaspoon of nutmeg, and a teaspoon of cinnamon. Pour this goo into the pie shell and bake at 400 degrees for about fifty minutes; make sure it's cooled down before attempting to serve. This also goes well with a shot of whipped cream.

One of the best and easiest pies I know about is actually a cross between a cheesecake and a key lime pie. It's rich and delicious, and any idiot can make it. In the cake mix section of the store, buy a premade graham cracker piecrust. Keebler makes them; they come in a foil pan with a plastic lid that can be removed and turned over to use later to protect the pie. Next to the Pet evaporated milk is something called Eagle brand sweetened condensed milk; you'll need one can. You'll also need a regulation-size package of cream cheese (the store's brand is just as good as Philly) and a small can of concentrated frozen lime juice. Leave the cream cheese out for an hour to soften it up. Then beat the hell out of it with a mixer. A big, standard mixer does better at this than one of the little hand mixers. (Point of information for the careful consumer: Big old Sunbeam mixers never wear out; I found a perfectly good one for $3 at a garage sale, beaters and mixing bowls included; or, you can pay $120 for a new one.) After beating the cream cheese for a while, pour in the Eagle brand milk. You'll need to scrape around the sides of the can with a rubber spatula to get all of this stuff out; it's sticky. Beat the cream cheese and the condensed milk together until the mixture is smooth. No kidding; there will be lumps in this stuff that have to be beaten out. Once you've gotten that all nice and creamy, toss in the frozen limeade and mix it well. At this point, I add a few drops of blue food coloring, mainly because the idea of a blue pie just really pisses my mother off. You can use green, or none, as you wish. Pour this all out into the graham cracker crust (having thoughtfully removed the plastic cover), scraping the mixing bowl well. Yes, you may lick the beaters. Refrigerate for two hours or so. This also is very rich, so serve small pieces. Great stuff. You can also serve this as individual tarts: Right next to the pie shells are little tinfoil pans with baby graham cracker crusts in them. Isn't that special?

So much for pie. If the meal you're serving is sort of slim pickin's (I did fillets of sole, broiled, the other night, counting on a strong finish with Mystic Mints; little did I know that Bob had hoovered them up that afternoon), come in strong with a nice big dessert. Now, this is a matter of strategy. You'll just get everybody bent out of shape if you feed them lasagne and then come in with dessert that's heavy as a rock. Stick with the sherbet in that case. But if you've not made your best effort with the meal itself, redemption can be found in strawberry shortcake. (I once overheard Judy muttering to herself as she was lopping the heads off a quart of strawberries in the sink, "I don't even *like* the little sons of bitches." At this point I knew the marriage was going to last.) The secret to strawberry shortcake is overabundance. Really. I mean, who wants just a little dab of strawberry shortcake? You either don't want any at all or you want a whole mess of it. So, plan on a pint of strawberries per two diners. A quart for four people; you get the idea. Lop their little green heads off (the strawberries', not the diners'), cut them in half, and then wash them in a colander. If you're also serving fruit salad, save a handful of the strawberries at this point to give it some color. Place the berries into a large bowl and pour two or three teaspoons of granulated sugar over them. Squash them lightly with a potato masher, just enough to break them up a bit and get the juice running; don't go mashing them down to mush. Refrigerate. This is where the plot thickens.

Remember Bisquick? The stuff in the yellow box, that's right. It's not only wonderful for biscuits and pancakes, but it is also the base for first-rate shortcake. The recipe is on the side of the box. It's basically Bisquick, melted butter, sugar, and a little milk. Once you've gotten it prepared and in the baking pan, sprinkle a bit of sugar over the top to give it a decorative, crunchy surface. Bake as directed on the box. With this stuff, it's perfectly acceptable (even preferable) to serve it while it's still hot out of the oven. Wait ten or fifteen minutes and then go to it. Smother with strawberries and whipped cream. Fall over on your side and keep eating.

It's also possible to do shortcake with peaches (either fresh or canned) or other kinds of fruits, even raspberries. Remember, enough of the aerosol whipped cream will cover up most any sort of mess. The main point is to bake the shortcake long enough; shortcake that's soggy in the middle is an abomination.

Now, it happens that since I started writing this brief book of help for the cooking-impaired, recipes from all sorts of friends, students, and relatives have been filtering down upon me. Many have not made the cut after rigorous trials in our vast complex of test kitchens. Mom, for example, is the person who really taught me how to cook, but she just hasn't gotten the concept of this book; all of her recipes take at least twelve ingredients and two or three hours to prepare. One dear lady gave me something that tasted just fine, but it started out, "Caramelize a cup and a half of sugar in a heavy pan, then separate six eggs. . . ." Hold it, hold it; I know my audience. We're talking *no-sweat* cookery here. Four or five ingredients, max. Nobody wants to make a career out of this.

Here are two quickies that fit into the idea of no-sweat cookery: Sheila King says melt a big package of almond bark (find it among the cake mixes at the store) along with a big package of chocolate chips. If you do this in the microwave, turn the bowl and stir every now and again. When it's melted, add a sixteen-ounce jar of salted dry-roasted peanuts; stir, and glob onto waxed paper with a teaspoon. When they've cooled, you've got dandy peanut clusters. That's the idea: easy and quick. Also, Janice Lovely's easy peachy cake: Dump a big can of sliced peaches, juice and all, into a nine-by-twelve-inch cake pan. Sprinkle over this an entire box of Betty Crocker Butterbrickle cake mix. Melt a stick of margarine and drizzle it over the cake mix; on top of that spread a cup of walnuts or pecans. Bake at 325 degrees for a half hour. Serve as you would a cobbler: still warm, with a glob of vanilla ice cream on top.

Now, the principle we have tried to emphasize all along throughout this book has been simplicity. The dessert, as the finale to a fine meal, should be simple as well. Buy a good cheesecake and pour a can of blueberry pie filling over the top of it. Give them vanilla ice cream with a dab of chocolate sauce. Don't let the preparation get away from you. Just mess around a little and be creative. There's nothing to be afraid of.

Unwilling to take over complete duties in the

kitchen? I don't blame you. On the other hand, don't be a lazy slug like my neighbor Richard. You can help out. While you're at it, teach your kids how to cook.

Cooking doesn't have to be a backbreaking job. If you study how to do things efficiently and go into it with the proper, positive frame of mind, you, too, may heal the sick, cleanse the leper, raise the dead, and cast out devils. There are great rewards for cooking, and it really is a no-sweat proposition.

Too many men are afraid to try. It's interesting that the people who have given me good cooking ideas are all women. Not *all* women hate men; there are still a few left who are willing to be helpful. Most men, though, have just sort of stood around and looked stupid when the topic of no-sweat cookery has come up. "Well . . . I'm not much of a cook. . . ." It's a crying shame. Men have been socialized to think that they'll fail in the kitchen, and this is a contemporary tragedy. The idea of certain things as "women's work" is dead and gone. Try a few things; act like you can fly. A little experimentation, starting off with something simple, just might lead to great things. Survival skills, even.

Men, you have nothing to lose but your chains.

Just be sure to clean up your mess.

Index

C

H

I

J

K

L

M

N

O

P

T